CONTENTS

**Targeting Homework
Year 2 New Edition**

Copyright © 2023 Blake Education
Reprinted 2024, 2025

ISBN: 978 1 92572 644 2

Published by Pascal Press
PO Box 250
Glebe NSW 2037
www.pascalpress.com.au
contact@pascalpress.com.au

Author: Norah Colvin
Publisher: Lynn Dickinson
Editor: Ruth Schultz
Cover and Text Designer: Leanne Nobilio
Typesetter: Ruth Schultz
Images & Illustrations: Dreamstime (unless otherwise indicated)

Printed by Wai Man Book Binding (China) Ltd

Acknowledgements
Thank you to the publishers, authors and illustrators
who generously granted permission for their work
to be reproduced in this book.

Introduction

Targeting Homework aims to build and reinforce English and Maths skills. This book supports the ACARA Australian Curriculum for Year 2 and helps children to revise and consolidate what has been taught in the classroom. ACARA codes are shown on each unit and a chart explaining their content descriptions is on pages v and vi. The inside back cover (Maths) and front cover (English) show the topics in each unit.

The structure of this book

This book has 32 carefully graded double-page units – 16 for English and 16 for Maths.

The English units are divided into three sections:

★ Grammar and Punctuation

★ Spelling and Phonic Knowledge

★ Reading and Comprehension — includes a wide variety of literary and cross-curriculum texts.

This also includes a Reading Review segment for children to record and rate their home reading books and some handwriting practice.

> **My Book Review**
>
> Title _____
>
> Author _____
>
> Colour stars to show your rating: ☆ ☆ ☆ ☆ ☆
>   Boring   Great!
>
> Comment _____
> _____

The Maths units are divided between:

★ Number and Algebra

★ Measurement and Space

★ Statistics

★ Problem Solving.

Assessment

Term Reviews follow Units 1–8, 9–16, 17–24 and 25–32 to test work covered during the term, and allow parents and carers to monitor their child's progress. Children are encouraged to mark each unit as it is completed and to colour in the traffic lights at the end of each segment. These results are then transferred to the Marking Grid. Parents and carers can see at a glance if their child is excelling or struggling!

● **Green** = Excellent — 2 or fewer questions incorrect
● **Orange** = Passing — 50% or more questions answered correctly
● **Red** = Struggling — fewer than 50% correct and needs help

SCORE **/18** (0-6) (8-14) (16-18)   *Score 2 points for each correct answer!*

How to Use This Book

The activities in this book are specifically designed to be used at home with minimal resources and support. Helpful explanations of key concepts and skills are provided throughout the book to help understand the tasks. Useful examples of how to do the activities are provided.

Regular practice of key concepts and skills will support the work your child does in school and will enable you to monitor their progress throughout the year. It is recommended that children complete 8 units per school term (one a week) and then the Term Review. Every unit has a Traffic Light scoreboard at the end of each section.

Score 2 points for each correct answer!

You or your child should mark each completed unit and then colour the traffic light that corresponds to the number of correct questions. This process will enable you to see at a glance how your child is progressing and to identify weak spots. The results should be recorded at the end of each term on the Marking Grid on page 1. The Term Review results are important for tracking progress and identifying any improvements in performance. If you find that certain questions are repeatedly causing difficulties and errors, then there is a good reason to discuss this with your child's teacher and arrange for extra instruction in that problem area.

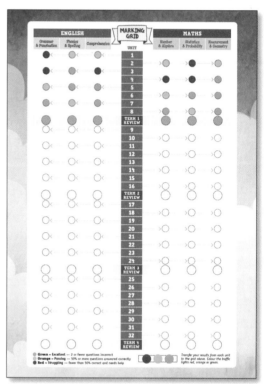

NOTE: The Maths Problem Solving questions do not appear on the Marking Grid as they often have multiple or subjective answers that cannot be easily scored.

Home Reading Journal

Each English unit provides space for your child to log, review and rate a book they have read during the week. These details can then be transferred to the handy Reading Journal Summary on page 146, which can be photocopied and shared with their teacher or kept as a record.

Answers

The answer section on pages 147–162 can be removed, stapled together and kept somewhere safe. Use it to check answers when your child has completed each unit. Encourage your child to colour in the Traffic Light boxes when the answers have been calculated.

TARGETING HOMEWORK 2 © PASCAL PRESS ISBN 9781925726442

Australian Curriculum Correlations: Year 2 English		Grammar & Punctuation	Phonic Knowledge & Spelling	Reading Comprehension
CODE	**CODE DESCRIPTION**	**UNITS**	**UNITS**	**UNITS**
LANGUAGE				
AC9E1LA06	Understand that a simple sentence consists of a single independent clause representing a single event or idea	1, 3, 5, 7		
AC9E1LA10	Understand that written language uses punctuation such as full stops, question marks and exclamation marks, and uses capital letters for familiar proper nouns	1, 3, 5		
AC9E2LA03	Identify how texts across the curriculum are organised differently and use language features depending on purposes			1, 3, 5, 7, 9, 11,13, 15, 17, 19, 21, 23, 25, 27, 29, 31
AC9E2LA05	Navigate print and screen texts using chapters, tables of contents, indexes, side-bar menus, drop-down menus or links	17, 19, 21, 23		15, 27
AC9E2LA06	Understand that connections can be made between ideas by using a compound sentence with 2 or more independent clauses usually linked by a coordinating conjunction	19, 21, 23		
AC9E2LA07	Understand that in sentences nouns may be extended into noun groups using articles and adjectives, and verbs may be expressed as verb groups	9, 11, 13, 17		
AC9E2LA08	Understand that images add to or multiply the meanings of a text			1, 3, 5, 7, 9, 11, 13, 15, 17, 19, 21, 23, 25, 27, 29, 31
AC9E2LA09	Experiment with and begin to make conscious choices of vocabulary to suit the topic	25, 27, 29, 31		
AC9E2LA10	Recognise that capital letters are used in titles and commas are used to separate items in lists	7, 13, 15		
LITERATURE				
AC9E2LE04	Identify, reproduce and experiment with rhythmic sound and word patterns in poems, chants, rhymes or songs			7, 21
LITERACY				
AC9E2LY03	Identify the purpose and audience of imaginative, informative and persuasive texts			7, 13, 15, 27, 31
AC9E2LY05	Use comprehension strategies such as visualising, predicting, connecting, summarising, monitoring and questioning to build literal and inferred meaning			1, 3, 5, 7, 9, 11, 13, 15, 17, 19, 21, 23, 25, 27, 29, 31
AC9E2LY08	Write words legibly and with growing fluency using unjoined upper-case and lower-case letters		1, 3, 7, 13, 15, 21, 23, 27, 29, 31	
AC9E2LY09	Manipulate more complex sounds in spoken words and use knowledge of blending, segmenting, phoneme deletion and phoneme substitution to read and write words		17, 19, 21	
AC9E2LY10	Use phoneme–grapheme (sound–letter/s) matches, including vowel digraphs, less common long vowel patterns, consonant clusters and silent letters when reading and writing words of one or more syllables, including compound words		1, 3, 5, 7, 9, 11, 13, 15, 17, 19, 21, 23, 25, 27, 29, 31	
AC9E2LY11	Use knowledge of spelling patterns and morphemes to read and write words whose spelling is not completely predictable from their sounds, including high frequency words		9, 11, 13, 15, 21, 23	
AC9E2LY12	Build morphemic word families using knowledge of prefixes and suffixes	13, 15	1, 3, 5, 7	

Australian CURRICULUM

Australian Curriculum Correlations: Year 2 Maths		Number & Algebra	Statistics	Measurement & Space	Problem Solving
CODE	CONTENT DESCRIPTION	UNITS	UNITS	UNITS	UNITS
NUMBER					
AC9M2N01	Recognise, represent and order numbers to at least 1000 using physical and virtual materials, numerals and number lines	2, 4, 6, 8, 10, 12, 14, 16, 18, 20, 22, 24, 26, 28, 30, 32			12, 18, 22, 26
AC9M2N02	Partition, rearrange, regroup and rename two- and three-digit numbers using standard and non-standard groupings; recognise the role of a zero digit in place value notation	6, 8, 10, 12, 14, 16, 18, 20, 22, 24, 26, 28, 30,			
AC9M2N03	Recognise and describe one-half as one of 2 equal parts of a whole and connect halves, quarters and eighths through repeated halving	8, 16, 24, 26, 32			
AC9M2N04	Add and subtract one- and two-digit numbers, representing problems using number sentences, and solve using part-part-whole reasoning and a variety of calculation strategies	2, 4, 6, 8, 12, 26, 32			
AC9M2N05	Multiply and divide by one-digit numbers using repeated addition, equal grouping, arrays, and partitioning to support a variety of calculation strategies	6, 10, 12, 14, 16, 18, 20, 22, 24, 28, 30, 32			
AC9M2N06	Use mathematical modelling to solve practical problems involving additive and multiplicative situations, including money transactions; represent situations and choose calculation strategies; interpret and communicate solutions in terms of the situation	6, 10, 12, 14, 16, 18, 20, 22, 24, 30			6, 8, 14, 20, 30
ALGEBRA					
AC9M2A01	Recognise, describe and create additive patterns that increase or decrease by a constant amount, using numbers, shapes and objects, and identify missing elements in the pattern	2, 4, 6, 8, 10, 12, 14, 16, 18, 20, 22, 24, 28, 30, 32			
AC9M2A02	Recall and demonstrate proficiency with addition facts to 20; extend and apply facts to develop related subtraction facts	2, 4, 6, 14, 24, 26			
AC9M2A03	Recall and demonstrate proficiency with multiplication facts for twos; extend and apply facts to develop the related division facts using doubling and halving	8, 10, 12, 14, 26, 28			
MEASUREMENT					
AC9M2M01	Measure and compare objects based on length, capacity and mass using appropriate uniform informal units and smaller units for accuracy when necessary		2, 18, 26		2
AC9M2M02	Identify common uses and represent halves, quarters and eighths in relation to shapes, objects and events		8, 12, 16, 24, 32		24, 32
AC9M2M03	Identify the date and determine the number of days between events using calendars		16, 24, 28		16
AC9M2M04	Recognise and read the time represented on an analog clock to the hour, half-hour and quarter-hour		4, 12, 20		4
AC9M2M05	Identify, describe and demonstrate quarter, half, three-quarter and full measures of turn in everyday situations		12, 20		
SPACE					
AC9M2SP01	Recognise, compare and classify shapes, referencing the number of sides and using spatial terms such as "opposite", "parallel", "curved" and "straight"		2, 10, 18, 20, 26, 28		10, 28
AC9M2SP02	Locate positions in two-dimensional representations of a familiar space; move positions by following directions and pathways		4, 12		26
STATISTICS					
AC9M2ST01	Acquire data for categorical variables through surveys, observation, experiment and using digital tools; sort data into relevant categories and display data using lists and tables			6, 8, 22, 30, 32	32
AC9M2ST02	Create different graphical representations of data using software where appropriate; compare the different representations, identify and describe common and distinctive features in response to questions			8, 14, 32	32

Australian CURRICULUM

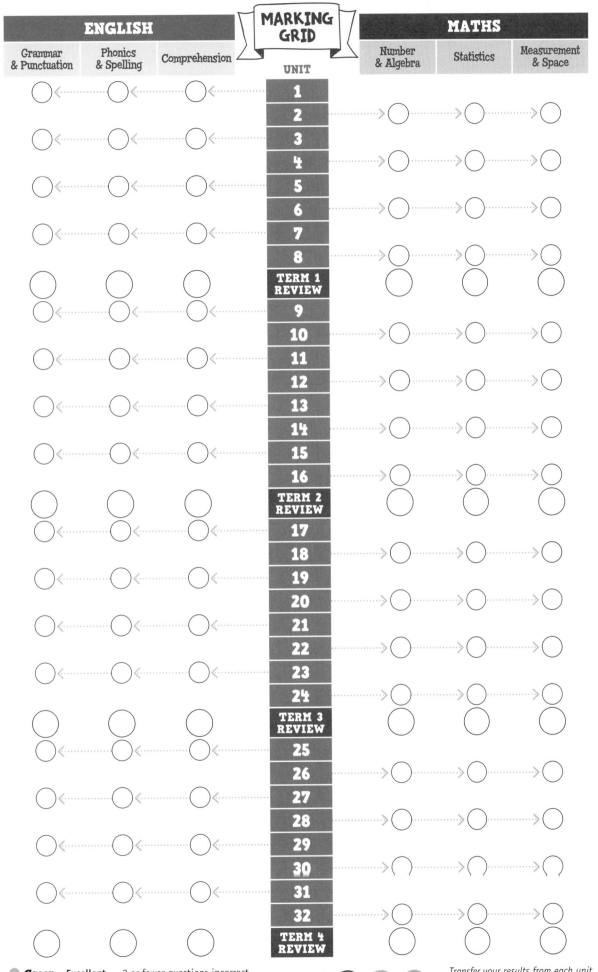

MARKING GRID

ENGLISH

Grammar & Punctuation | Phonics & Spelling | Comprehension

MATHS

Number & Algebra | Statistics | Measurement & Space

UNIT

1
2
3
4
5
6
7
8
TERM 1 REVIEW
9
10
11
12
13
14
15
16
TERM 2 REVIEW
17
18
19
20
21
22
23
24
TERM 3 REVIEW
25
26
27
28
29
30
31
32
TERM 4 REVIEW

● **Green** = Excellent — 2 or fewer questions incorrect
● **Orange** = Passing — 50% or more questions answered correctly
● **Red** = Struggling — fewer than 50% correct and needs help

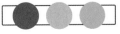

Transfer your results from each unit to the grid above. Colour the traffic lights red, orange or green.

Grammar & Punctuation

AC9EILA06, AC9EILA10

Sentences

> A **sentence** is a group of words that makes sense on its own.
> A sentence begins with a **capital letter** and ends with a **full stop**.

Read the groups of words. Write S if it is a sentence.
Draw a cross if it is not a sentence.

① _____ a flock of birds

② _____ A boy ran down the road.

③ _____ Joseph Banks

④ _____ a funny clown

⑤ _____ A bird flew high over the water.

⑥ _____ before school

⑦ _____ I went to the beach.

⑧ _____ after the rain

Draw lines to match the sentence beginnings and endings.

⑨ The girl in the green shirt   make sure you have everything you need.

⑩ After the rain stopped,   for our holidays.

⑪ Before you go home,   came first in the race.

⑫ We went to the beach   the sun came out.

Write more words to finish the sentences.

⑬ The red car _____.

⑭ The big brown horse _____.

⑮ The frightened child _____.

⑯ The blue balloon _____.

⑰ The enormous crocodile _____.

Verbs are action words or being words. They tell what is happening in a sentence.
Circle the verbs in these sentences. They tell what is happening now.

⑱ The angry farmer chases the crows out of her corn.

⑲ The tiny plant grows bigger and bigger and bigger.

⑳ The happy children dance to the music.

㉑ The bird flies to the top of the tree.

Score 2 points for each correct answer! **SCORE** /42 (0-18) (20-36) (38-42)

TARGETING HOMEWORK 2 © PASCAL PRESS ISBN 9781925726442

TERM 1 ENGLISH

Adding endings to verbs

We add endings to verbs to show **when** things happen. We add **ing** to show that the action **continues**. We add **ed** to show that the action happened in the **past**.

Add ing and ed to these words.

		+ ing	+ ed
①	watch	_____	_____
②	crack	_____	_____
③	wish	_____	_____
④	look	_____	_____

Long vowel sounds – e on the end

When a word has an e **on the end**, the other vowel often makes the **long vowel sound**.

Read the words. Write an e on the end. Then read the new word.

⑤ cap___   ⑦ man___   ⑨ rid___   ⑪ kit___

⑥ rod___   ⑧ not___   ⑩ cub___   ⑫ hug___

Choose a word from the box at the right to complete these sentences.

⑬ The horse has a long _____.

⑭ The children watched the _____ fly high in the sky.

⑮ The lost puppy couldn't find its way _____.

⑯ They couldn't play the game because they ran out of _____.

⑰ The _____ slug left a slimy trail over the footpath.

| home |
| huge |
| kite |
| mane |
| time |

Cross out the incorrect word in each sentence.

⑱ The children had a **rid ride** on a horse at the farm.

⑲ The old man used a **can cane** to help him walk.

⑳ My mother wrote a **not note** to the teacher.

㉑ Dad used a **mop mope** to clean the floor.

㉒ A dice is in the shape of a **cub cube**.

Score 2 points for each correct answer!

SCORE **/44**   (0-20)   (22-38)   (40-44)

Trace the words. Start at the star. Follow the arrows.

The boy in a cape rode his bike home.

TERM 1 ENGLISH

Reading & Comprehension

AC9E2LA03, AC9E2LA08, AC9E2LY05

Imaginative text – Narrative

The Best Seats

Lady Coco Rose and her dog, Tinks, wanted the best seats in the circus.

When Wonderful Wilma came out with her lions, they were in the front row but they wanted to be even closer.

Lady Coco spotted two stools in the ring.

"They are the best seats in the circus!" she cried.

Lady Coco rushed to grab them.

"I'm sorry," said the Ringmaster, "But they are already taken!"

Source: Storylands Circus Bizurkus, *The Best Seats*, Blake Education

Write or tick the correct answer.

① Where did Lady Coco Rose and her dog go?

☐ **a** the zoo ☐ **b** the theatre ☐ **c** the circus ☐ **d** the show

② What was the name of the dog?

☐ **a** Coco ☐ **b** Tinks ☐ **c** Rose ☐ **d** Wilma

TARGETING HOMEWORK 2 © PASCAL PRESS ISBN 9781925726442

③ Where was Lady Coco sitting when the lions came out?

_____

④ Who is Wonderful Wilma?

☐ **a** the lion tamer

☐ **b** the ringmaster

☐ **c** Lady Coco's friend

☐ **d** another person watching the show

⑤ What is the ring where Lady Coco saw two stools?

☐ **a** a wedding ring

☐ **b** a ring of children

☐ **c** the place where circus acts are performed

☐ **d** a hoop

⑥ Why did Lady Coco say the stools were the best seats?

☐ **a** They were closer.

☐ **b** They were more comfortable.

☐ **c** They were further away.

☐ **d** They were higher.

⑦ Who were the stools for?

_____

⑧ What does the ringmaster mean when he says the stools are 'taken'?

☐ **a** They were taken out of the tent.

☐ **b** They were taken from the stand to the ring.

☐ **c** They were already being used.

☐ **d** They were taken apart.

⑨ What happened when Lady Coco rushed to grab the stools?

☐ **a** The lions roared at her.

☐ **b** She slipped over.

☐ **c** She sat on the stools with her dog Tinks.

☐ **d** She took the stools home.

⑩ What do you think Lady Coco did when the lions roared at her?

_____

_____

Score 2 points for each correct answer! **SCORE** **/20** (0-8) (10-14) (16-20)

My Book Review

Title _____

Author _____

Colour stars to show your rating: ☆ ☆ ☆ ☆ ☆

　　　　　　　Boring　　　　　　　　　Great!

Comment _____

_____

Counting in twos

① Continue the jumps **in 2s** on the number line.

+ 2

0 1 2 3 4 5 6 7 8 9 10 11 12 13 14 15 16

Write the missing numbers.
Circle F for counting forwards. Circle B for counting backwards.

②

| 16 | | 20 | | 24 | | | | 32 | |

F   B

③

| 62 | | | | 72 | | | | 80 |

F   B

④

| 50 | | 46 | | | | 38 | | | |

F   B

⑤

| 88 | 86 | | | | | | 74 | | |

F   B

Write these numbers in order from **smallest to largest**.

⑥ 27, 17, 72, 65, 56

_____, _____, _____, _____, _____

⑦ 63, 60, 16, 61, 96

_____, _____, _____, _____, _____

Write these numbers in order from **largest to smallest**.

⑧ 99, 66, 96, 16, 69

_____, _____, _____, _____, _____

⑨ 55, 58, 85, 18, 81

_____, _____, _____, _____, _____

⑩ Circle the number **closest to 100**. Underline the number **closest to 0**.

59   95   45   29   15   37   64   87   21   9

Write the two addition turnaround facts for each domino.

⑪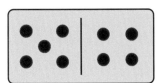

_____ + _____ = _____

_____ + _____ = _____

⑬

_____ + _____ = _____

_____ + _____ = _____

⑫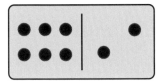

_____ + _____ = _____

_____ + _____ = _____

⑭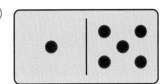

_____ + _____ = _____

_____ + _____ = _____

Use addition to work out the answer.

⑮ Jess and Lara were comparing how many goals they scored on the weekend.
Jess said, "I scored five goals."
Lara said, "I scored three more than you."

How many goals did Lara score?_____

⑯ Look at these dice. The numbers total 11.
How many dots are on the second dice?
Show how you worked it out.

_____

⑰ Look at these dice. The numbers total 9.
How many dots are on the second dice?
Show how you worked it out.

_____

⑱ You need to roll exactly 10 to win the game.
If you roll 5 on the first dice, how many do you need to roll on the second dice?

_____

⑲ You need to roll exactly 7 to win the game.
If you roll 4 on the first dice, how many do you need to roll on the second dice?

_____

Score 2 points
for each
correct answer!   SCORE   /38

TARGETING HOMEWORK 2 © PASCAL PRESS ISBN 9781925726442

7

Length

You need some 5c coins.
Use the coins to measure the length of each object.
How many coins do you need?

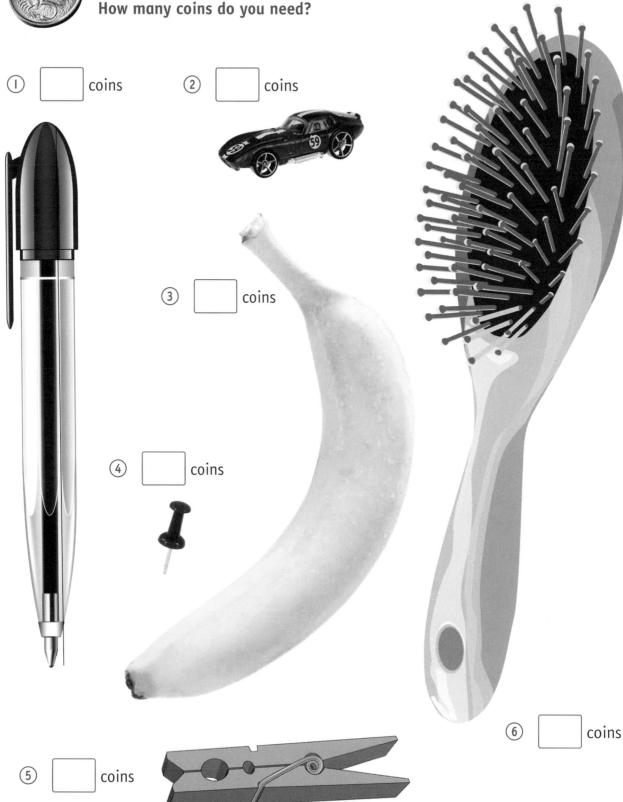

① ☐ coins

② ☐ coins

③ ☐ coins

④ ☐ coins

⑤ ☐ coins

⑥ ☐ coins

⑦ Now use the coins to measure the height of this page: _____ coins

⑧ Now measure the width of this page: _____ coins

TARGETING HOMEWORK 2 © PASCAL PRESS ISBN 9781925726442

Straight and curved lines

Some **lines** are **straight**, like these:

Some **lines** are **curved**, like these:

Some shapes are made of only straight lines. Some shapes are made of only curved lines.
Some shapes are made of both straight lines and curved lines.

Use **blue** to colour the shapes made of only **straight** lines.
Use **yellow** to colour the shapes made of only **curved** lines.
Use **green** to colour the shapes made of both **straight** and **curved** lines.
Write words to describe the lines.

⑨ _____

⑪ _____

⑬ _____

⑩ _____

⑫ _____

⑭ _____

Score 2 points for each correct answer! **SCORE** **/ 28** (0-12) (14-22) (24-28)

Problem Solving

AC9M2M01

① You need some clothes pegs.
How many pegs do you need
to measure the length of your table?

First estimate the answer: ⬜ pegs   **Now measure:** ⬜ pegs

② You need some building blocks.
Make sure they are all the same length.
How many blocks do you need to measure the height of your table?

First estimate the answer: ⬜ blocks   **Now measure:** ⬜ blocks

TERM 1 MATHS

Statements

> A **statement** is a sentence that **gives information**.
>
> **The girl kicked the ball.**
>
> A statement begins with a **capital letter** and ends with a **full stop**.
>
> A **question** is a sentence that **asks for information**.
>
> **Who kicked the ball?**
>
> A question begins with a **capital letter** and ends with a **question mark**.

Read these sentences. Write S for statement. Write Q for question.

① _____ Where did you play football today?

② _____ Why did you say that?

③ _____ What was that noise I heard?

④ _____ Who took the last apple?

⑤ _____ I stayed at home on the weekend.

⑥ _____ The children played chase.

⑦ _____ Where did you put my toys?

⑧ _____ I went to the beach on Saturday.

⑨ _____ When did you see the movie?

Questions often begin with words like who, what, where, when, why and how.

Read this sentence: The children went to the beach on the weekend.

Write questions about this sentence. Put a question mark at the end of each one.

⑩ Who _____

⑪ What _____

⑫ Where _____

⑬ When _____

⑭ Why _____

⑮ How _____

Score 2 points for each correct answer! **SCORE** **/ 30** 0-12 14-24 26-30

TARGETING HOMEWORK 2 © PASCAL PRESS ISBN 9781925726442

Phonic Knowledge & Spelling

AC9E2LY08, AC9E2LY10, AC9E2LY12

Adding endings to verbs

> We add endings to verbs to show **when** things happen. We add **ing** to show that the action **continues.** We add **ed** to show that the action happened in the **past.**
>
> We just add **ing** or **ed** when a word has **two vowels,** as in look and leak, or ends with **two consonants,** as in wish and kick.

Write the word and its correct ending to finish the sentence.

① **look**   The girl was _____ at trees in the playground.

② **paint**   The artist _____ some beautiful sunflowers.

③ **climb**   The monkeys were _____ in the trees.

④ **plant**   I _____ some carrots in our garden.

⑤ **pack**   The girl _____ her bag for school.

⑥ **guess**   I _____ the correct answer.

Long vowel sounds – long a

There are different ways of spelling the long a sound.
Read these words. Cross out the word that doesn't have the long a vowel sound.

⑦   baby   lady   happy   navy

⑧   snail   pail   trail   tall

⑨   eight   freight   weight   height

⑩   they   key   prey   grey

Long vowel sounds – long e

There are different ways of spelling the long e sound.
Read these words. Cross out the word that doesn't have the long e vowel sound.

⑪   emu   equal   eleven   egg

⑫   meat   head   beach   cream

⑬   see   tree   fried   free

⑭   key   monkey   grey   honey

Choose one of the long a or long e words on this page to complete the sentences.

⑮   The tiny _____ made a long trail across the path.

⑯   Ten plus ten is _____ to twenty.

⑰   The sky was dark with _____ clouds.

⑱   The pirate lost the _____ to her treasure chest.

Score 2 points for each correct answer!   **SCORE**   **/36**   0-16   18-30   32-36

TERM 1 ENGLISH

The lady made a cake with cream and honey.

TERM 1 ENGLISH

Reading & Comprehension

Informative text – Table and Graph

AC9E2LA03, AC9E2LA08, AC9E2LY05

Animal Species

There are millions of different species of animals in the world.

Animal group	Number of species (approx.)
Vertebrates	
Fish	30 000
Amphibians	6 200
Birds	10 000
Mammals	5 400
Reptiles	8 200
Invertebrates	
Insects	950 000
Others	253 000

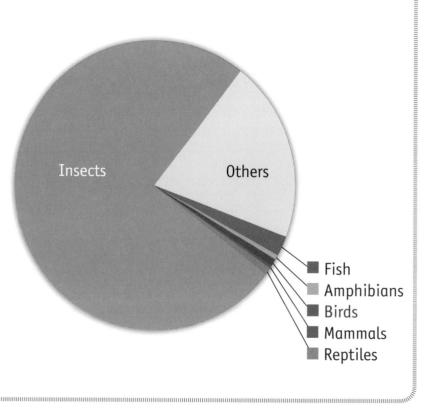

Source: Steve Parish First Facts, *Birds*, Pascal Press

Write or tick the correct answer.

1. Which animal group has the most species?

   ☐ **a** fish ☐ **c** birds

   ☐ **b** insects ☐ **d** mammals

2. The animals listed as 'others' are

   ☐ **a** vertebrates.

   ☐ **b** invertebrates.

   ☐ **c** unidentified animals.

3. On the graph, mosquitoes would belong to which group?

   ☐ **a** insects ☐ **c** fish

   ☐ **b** reptiles ☐ **d** others

4. The number of species is 'Approx.' What does this mean?

   ☐ **a** about ☐ **c** exactly

   ☐ **b** more than ☐ **d** less than

5. The animal group with the smallest number of species is

   ☐ **a** insects. ☐ **c** mammals.

   ☐ **b** amphibians. ☐ **d** reptiles.

6. Are there more species of vertebrates or invertebrates?

   _____

7. Which group of vertebrates has the most species?

   ☐ **a** mammals ☐ **c** fish

   ☐ **b** amphibians ☐ **d** birds

8. What colour is used to show fish on the graph?

   ☐ **a** red ☐ **c** green

   ☐ **b** orange ☐ **d** purple

9. What species is shown by orange on the graph?

   ☐ **a** amphibians ☐ **c** mammals

   ☐ **b** fish ☐ **d** insects

10. Which animal group has 8200 species?

    ☐ **a** reptiles ☐ **c** fish

    ☐ **b** birds ☐ **d** mammals

Score 2 points for each correct answer! SCORE **/ 20** (0-8) (10-14) (16-20)

My Book Review

Title _____

Author _____

Colour stars to show your rating: ☆ ☆ ☆ ☆ ☆

Boring   Great!

Comment _____

_____

Number & Algebra

AC9M2N01, AC9M2N04, AC9M2A01, AC9M2A02

Counting in threes

Look at this 100 grid.

① Colour the numbers to count in **threes**.
The first one is done for you.

1	2	3	4	5	6	7	8	9	10
11	12	13	14	15	16	17	18	19	20
21	22	23	24	25	26	27	28	29	30
31	32	33	34	35	36	37	38	39	40
41	42	43	44	45	46	47	48	49	50
51	52	53	54	55	56	57	58	59	60
61	62	63	64	65	66	67	68	69	70
71	72	73	74	75	76	77	78	79	80
81	82	83	84	85	86	87	88	89	90
91	92	93	94	95	96	97	98	99	100

TERM 1 MATHS

Write the missing numbers.
Circle F for counting forwards.
Circle B for counting backwards.

② | 12 | 15 | 18 | | | 30 | | | 39 | | F   B

③ | 60 | 57 | 54 | | | 39 | | | | F   B

④ | 69 | | 75 | | 84 | | | | 99 | F   B

⑤ | 78 | | | | 63 | 60 | | | 51 | | F   B

Write the number that is 3 more.

⑥ 32 _____   ⑦ 53 _____   ⑧ 17 _____

Write the number that is 3 less.

⑨ 78 _____   ⑩ 45 _____   ⑪ 99 _____

⑫ Write these numbers in order, from **smallest** to **largest**.

68   88   18   86   81   27   31   13

_____, _____, _____, _____, _____, _____, _____, _____

⑬ Write these numbers in order, from **largest** to **smallest**.

42   18   9   65   92   29   38   54

_____, _____, _____, _____, _____, _____, _____, _____

TARGETING HOMEWORK 2 © PASCAL PRESS ISBN 9781925726442

Count in **tens**. Write how many buttons altogether.

⑭ [ ]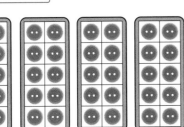

⑯ [ ]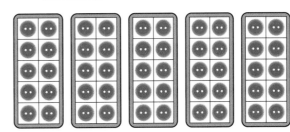

⑮ [ ]

⑰ [ ]

Some buttons are missing from the tens frames.
Write an **addition fact** and a **subtraction fact** for each frame.

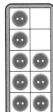

⑱ _____ + _____ = 10

⑲ 10 – _____ = _____

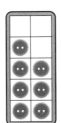

⑳ _____ + _____ = 10

㉑ 10 – _____ = _____

Read these number stories. Use addition or subtraction to find the answer.
Write the addition or subtraction fact you used.

㉒ Lara scored 5 goals in the first half
and 2 goals in the second half.
How many goals did Lara score altogether? _____

㉓ Tema saved $5 to buy a book.
His mum gave him $4 more.
How much money does Tema have now? _____

㉔ Jess made 10 cupcakes. She ate 3.
How many cupcakes does Jess have now? _____

㉕ Sam had 9 toy cars. He gave 5 to Zayne.
How many toy cars does Sam have now? _____

Score 2 points
for each
correct answer!
SCORE | **/50** | 0-22 | 24-44 | 46-50

TERM 1 MATHS

Interpret a map

Your friend Eva and her family have come to beach near where you live for a holiday. They are staying in the hotel marked with an **X**.

You and Eva decide to explore the rocks for crabs and other creatures.
You made this map to show Eva how to get there. But first she needs to buy a new hat.

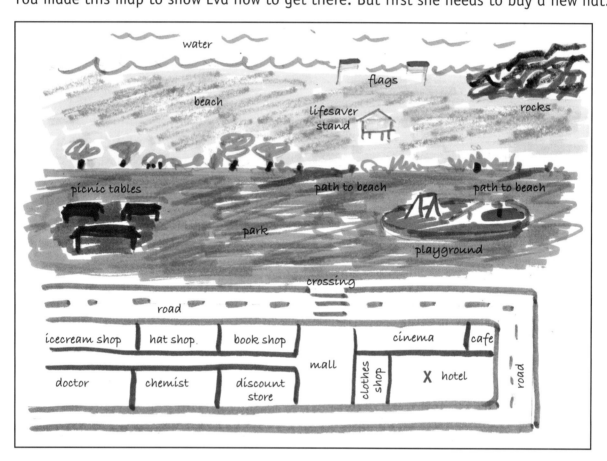

① Draw the path Eva will take from her hotel to the rocks.
   Make sure she stops to buy a hat on the way.

List four things Eva will see on the way, in order.

② _____   ④ _____

③ _____   ⑤ _____

⑥ Name one thing Eva will need to go through. _____

⑦ Name one thing Eva will need to cross over. _____

⑧ Which direction will Eva turn when she gets to the beach? _____

⑨ What could you and Eva do after you explore the rocks? List three ideas.

_____

_____

When the **big hand** is pointing straight up to the **12**, it is **o'clock**. The **little hand** tells **what o'clock** it is.

When the **big hand** points straight down to **6**, it has gone **halfway** around the clock from 12. It is **half past** the hour. The **little hand** has moved past the hour and is halfway to the next number.

2 o'clock

half past 2

Look at these clocks. Write the time you see.

⑩

⑪

⑫

⑬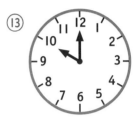

_____   _____   _____   _____

Draw the missing hand to show the time.

⑭ half past 5

⑮ 9 o'clock

⑯ 1 o'clock

⑰ half past 10

Draw the hands to show the time.

⑱ 3 o'clock

⑲ half past 7

Score 2 points for each correct answer!

SCORE /38 0-16 18-32 34-38

Problem Solving

AC9M2M04

Three friends were going to the beach.
Ari went by bus. Beth went by car. Zoe rode a bike.

It took the bus two hours to get there.
It took the car one hour.
It took the bike one and a half hours.

① If they all left home at 1 o'clock, who arrived at the beach first? _____

② What time did the first person arrive? _____

Requests and commands

A **request** is a type of question. It asks for something, or for someone to do something. Requests often use the word **please**. The answer might be yes or no.

Can I have a piece of cake, please?   Will you close the window, please?

A **command** tells you what to do. Unlike a request, you may not say yes or no. You must do it. Some commands end with a **full stop**. Some end with an **exclamation mark**.

Give me the cake.   Close the window!

Read these sentences. Write R if the sentence is a request. Write C if it is a command.

① ____ Shut the door!

② ____ Will you tie my shoelaces, please?

③ ____ Can I play with you?

④ ____ Will you help me with my homework, please?

⑤ ____ Finish your homework before you turn on the TV.

⑥ ____ Close your books and put your pencils down.

⑦ ____ Will you read me a story, please?

⑧ ____ Eat your vegetables first.

⑨ ____ May I go outside now?

⑩ ____ Stop doing that!

Read these requests. Rewrite them as commands.

⑪ Will you open the door, please?

_____

⑫ Will you turn off the light, please?

_____

⑬ Will you help me wash the car, please?

_____

⑭ Will you take the bin outside, please?

_____

⑮ Will you take the dog for a walk?

_____

Score 2 points for each correct answer!

SCORE / 30   0-12   14-24   26-30

TARGETING HOMEWORK 2 © PASCAL PRESS ISBN 9781925726442

Adding endings to verbs

We add endings to verbs to show **when** things happen. We add **ing** to show that the action **continues**. We add **ed** to show that the action happened in the **past**.

When a word **ends with e**, cross off the e before you add **ing** or **ed**:
   bake, **bak**ing, **bak**ed   **car**e, **car**ing, **car**ed

When a word ends with the **vowel y**, just add **ing** but change the **y to i** before you add **ed**:
   try, **try**ing, **tri**ed   **worry**, **worry**ing, **worri**ed

Add ing and ed to these words. Remember the rules!

		+ ing	+ ed
①	tape	_____	_____
②	like	_____	_____
③	smile	_____	_____
④	change	_____	_____
⑤	dry	_____	_____
⑥	copy	_____	_____
⑦	tidy	_____	_____
⑧	fry	_____	_____

Long vowel sounds – long i

There are different ways of spelling the long i sound.
Read these words. Cross out the word that doesn't have the long i vowel sound.

⑨ fine mite fin ride

⑩ high sign eight might

⑪ tiger tyre bright bigger

⑫ pie pit by buy

⑬ tray try cry fly

Long vowel sounds – long o

There are different ways of spelling the long o sound.
Read these words. Cross out the word that doesn't have the long o vowel sound.

⑭ no note not nose

⑮ stone bone tone shone

⑯ show though sew now

⑰ boat toad rod rose

⑱ down flow glow grow

Score 2 points for each correct answer!

SCORE **/36** (0-16) (18-30) (32-36)

TERM 1 ENGLISH

AC9E2LA03, AC9E2LA08, AC9E2LY05

Imaginative text – Narrative

The Great Show Starter

Colin really wanted to join a circus.

But his friends and teachers at circus school were not so sure.

No matter how hard he tried, there wasn't anything he could do well enough until ...

One day, the animals let Colin join their secret music game.
The animals found out how Colin could join a circus!

The animals made Colin a special suit. They helped him practise his act.
Then they called Ringmaster Ray.

Circus Bizurkus arrived and the whole circus school came out to watch.

Out came Colin in his musical suit. Colin's act began as a tap, tap, tap
and quickly turned into a boom, boom, boom.

A bounce was a bang and a step was a shake.
His suit strummed when he strutted.
When he wriggled it rocked.

"We must have Colin's crazy musical
act!" everyone cried.

"Welcome to Circus Bizurkus,"
said Ringmaster Roy. "You
shall be our opening act!"

Source: Storylands Circus Bizurkus, *The Great Show Starter*, Blake Education

Write or tick the correct answer.

① What did Colin do so he could join the circus?

- ☐ **a** He ran away from home.
- ☐ **b** He went to circus school.
- ☐ **c** He joined a band.
- ☐ **d** He asked the ringmaster.

② At first, Colin's friends and teachers thought

- ☐ **a** that Colin was good at everything.
- ☐ **b** that Colin would make a good animal trainer.
- ☐ **c** that Colin wasn't very good at circus tricks.
- ☐ **d** that Colin was a trouble maker.

TARGETING HOMEWORK 2 © PASCAL PRESS ISBN 9781925726442

③ What did Colin play with the animals?

- [ ] **a** hide and seek
- [ ] **b** catch me if you can
- [ ] **c** a circus game
- [ ] **d** secret music

④ How did Colin join the circus?

- [ ] **a** He became an animal trainer.
- [ ] **b** He became the ringmaster.
- [ ] **c** He played music.
- [ ] **d** He begged everyone to let him.

⑤ What was special about the way Colin made music?

- [ ] **a** He wore a special musical suit.
- [ ] **b** The animals played in his band.
- [ ] **c** He liked to play the drums.
- [ ] **d** The whole circus school listened.

⑥ Who watched Colin perform his music?

- [ ] **a** the circus school
- [ ] **b** Circus Bizurkus
- [ ] **c** the animals
- [ ] **d** all of the above

⑦ Did the audience like Colin's music?

- [ ] **a** yes
- [ ] **b** no

⑧ How do you think Colin's friends and teachers felt when he played his music?

- [ ] **a** surprised
- [ ] **c** annoyed
- [ ] **b** proud
- [ ] **d** jealous

⑨ How do you think Colin felt when everyone cheered his act?

- [ ] **a** surprised
- [ ] **c** annoyed
- [ ] **b** proud
- [ ] **d** jealous

⑩ When will Colin perform at the circus?

- [ ] **a** at the beginning of the show
- [ ] **b** at the end of the show
- [ ] **c** when the lions are performing
- [ ] **d** all through the show

Score 2 points for each correct answer!

SCORE **/20** (0-8) (10-14) (16-20)

My Book Review

Title _____

Author _____

Colour stars to show your rating: ☆ ☆ ☆ ☆ ☆

Boring   Great!

Comment _____

_____

TARGETING HOMEWORK 2 © PASCAL PRESS ISBN 9781925726442

Counting in fives

Count the number of fingers in fives. Write the numbers as you count.

①

____, ____, ____, ____, ____, ____, ____, ____, ____, ____, ____, ____, ____, ____

② Each box has five marbles. Count the marbles in fives.
Write the numbers on the boxes as you count.

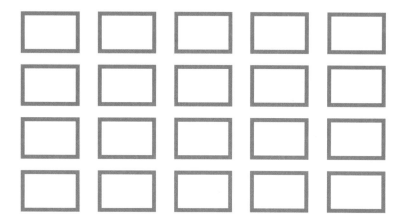

Write the missing numbers.
Circle **F** for counting **forwards**. Circle **B** for counting **backwards**.

③ | 5 | 10 | | | | 35 | | | F   B |

④ | 50 | | 40 | | | | 15 | | F   B |

⑤ | 85 | 80 | | | | 55 | | | F   B |

Look at these tens frames and buttons.
Count in tens, then add the extra buttons. Write how many altogether.

⑥ [ ]   ⑦ [ ]   ⑧ [ ]

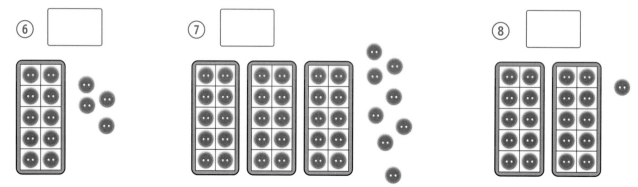

TARGETING HOMEWORK 2 © PASCAL PRESS ISBN 9781925726442

TERM 1 MATHS

Write two addition facts and two subtraction facts for each of these dominoes.

⑨ _____ + _____ = _____

⑩ _____ + _____ = _____

⑪ _____ − _____ = _____

⑫ _____ − _____ = _____

⑬ _____ + _____ = _____

⑭ _____ + _____ = _____

⑮ _____ − _____ = _____

⑯ _____ − _____ = _____

Use the **count on 1** or **count on 2** strategy to complete these **additions**.

⑰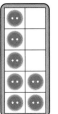

_____ , _____ , _____

⑱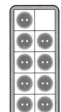

_____ , _____

Use the **count back 1** or **count back 2** strategy to complete these **subtractions**.

⑲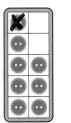

_____ , _____

⑳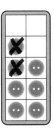

_____ , _____ , _____

Money

Look at the coins.

㉑ Use green to colour the coin with the greatest value.

㉒ Use red to colour the coin with the smallest value.

㉓ Tick the coin that is largest in size.

㉔ Cross the coin that is smallest in size.

Circle coins to make up the same value as the first coin.

㉕

㉖

Number & Algebra

(27)

(28)

(29)

(30)

(31) Count the total value of these coins.

Score 2 points for each correct answer!

SCORE / 62 (0-28) (30-56) (58-62)

Statistics

AC9M2ST01

Asking questions and gathering data

A class worked in groups to investigate questions. They made these graphs.

Group 1 _____   Group 2 _____

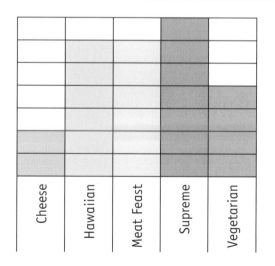

| Magpies | Myna birds | Crows | Cockatoos | Kookaburras |

| Cheese | Hawaiian | Meat Feast | Supreme | Vegetarian |

TARGETING HOMEWORK 2 © PASCAL PRESS ISBN 9781925726442

Group 3 _____

Group 4 _____

				Soccer

Soccer	Hockey	Netball	Tennis	Rugby League

White	Black	Red	Blue	Green

TERM 1 MATHS

Here are the questions the class investigated.
Write the correct question above each graph.

① What is your favourite sport?

② What birds will we see in the yard?

③ What is your favourite pizza?

④ What colour cars will go by?

Write the number of the group – 1, 2, 3 or 4 – that could answer the question.
Then answer the question.

⑤ Were there more green cars than white cars? Group: ___ Answer: _____

⑥ What pizza was the class favourite? Group: ___ Answer: _____

⑦ Which birds did we see most of? Group: ___ Answer: _____

⑧ What is the least favourite sport? Group: ___ Answer: _____

⑨ How many kookaburras did we see? Group: ___ Answer: _____

⑩ How many children prefer vegetarian pizza? Group: ___ Answer: _____

⑪ How many cars did we see? Group: ___ Answer: _____

⑫ Which groups interviewed all the children in the class? _____

Score 2 points for each correct answer!

SCORE **/24** (0-10) (12-18) (20-24)

Problem Solving

AC9M2N06

Tema wants to buy a ball that costs $2.35.
Circle the coins he could use to buy it.

$2.35

Grammar & Punctuation

AC9EILA06, AC9E2LA10

Using commas in lists

In a sentence, use commas in between the items in a **list**. Like this:

For our fruit salad, we need strawberries, pineapple, apple, oranges and kiwi fruit.

Use the word **and** before the last item, instead of a comma.

TERM 1 ENGLISH

Add the missing commas.

① For breakfast, I had eggs bacon mushroom tomatoes and toast.

② Sam invited Mark Tema Zayne Jess and Sarah to his party.

③ I used paper cardboard glue and paint to make my toy boat.

④ The shop was selling books cards wrapping paper and other gifts.

Write the list of items in a sentence to tell what the children took to camp.

⑤ **Sam**   paper   pencils   a scrapbook   sticky tape

_____

_____

⑥ **Sarah**   a hat   gloves   a mask   sunglasses   insect spray

_____

_____

⑦ **Tema**   a book   a torch   a pillow

_____

_____

⑧ **Jess**   a butterfly net   a magnifying glass   tweezers   two notebooks

_____

_____

⑨ **Zayne**   goggles   sunscreen   a rashie   flippers

_____

_____

Score 2 points for each correct answer!   **SCORE**   **/18**   (0-6)   (8-14)   (16-18)

TARGETING HOMEWORK 2 © PASCAL PRESS ISBN 9781925726442

Adding endings to verbs

We add endings to verbs to show **when** things happen. We add **ing** to show that the action **continues**. We add **ed** to show that the action happened in the **past**.

When a word has **one vowel and one consonant** at the end, **double the consonant** before you add **ing** or **ed**:

hug, **hug**ged, **hug**ging   stop, stopping, stopped

Add ing and ed to these words. Remember to double the consonant.

		+ ing	+ ed
①	tip	_____	_____
②	rob	_____	_____
③	grab	_____	_____
④	jog	_____	_____

Write the word and its correct ending to finish the sentence.

⑤ **clap**   The children _____ when the show ended.

⑥ **plan**   The children are _____ to have a party on the weekend.

⑦ **skip**   The girls _____ to the shop.

⑧ **hop**   The boy was _____ on one leg as fast as he could.

Long vowel sounds – long u

The long u sound sounds like **you** and there are **different ways of spelling it**.
Tick the words that have the **long u vowel sound**. Cross the other words.

⑨ ☐ fun   ⑫ ☐ cub   ⑮ ☐ cute   ⑱ ☐ tub

⑩ ☐ huge   ⑬ ☐ tube   ⑯ ☐ us   ⑲ ☐ cube

⑪ ☐ music   ⑭ ☐ use   ⑰ ☐ few   ⑳ ☐ cut

Choose words from the activity above to complete these sentences.

㉑   The children played _____ in the concert for their parents.

㉒   The _____ elephant was almost as tall as the tree.

㉓   The old man played with the _____ little kitten.

Score 2 points for each correct answer!   SCORE   **/46**   (0-20)   (22-40)   (42-46)

Trace the words. Start at the star. Follow the arrows.

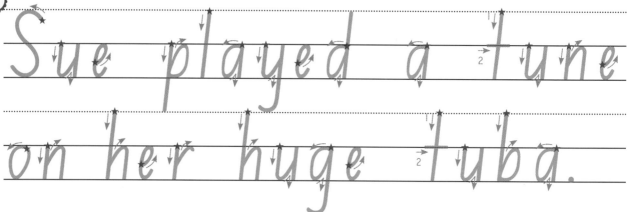

Sue played a tune

on her huge tuba.

TERM 1 ENGLISH

Reading & Comprehension

AC9E2LA03, AC9E2LA08, AC9E2LE04, AC9E2LY03, AC9E2LY05

Imaginative text – Nonsense Poetry

There was an Old Man with a Beard
by Edward Lear

There was an Old Man with a beard,

Who said, "It is just as I feared! —

Two Owls and a Hen, four Larks and a Wren,

Have all built their nests in my beard."

Illustrator: Paul Lennon

Write or tick the correct answer.

① How would you describe the old man in the poem?

◻ **a** He was a farmer.

◻ **b** He didn't like animals.

◻ **c** He had a beard.

◻ **d** He had a nest for a beard.

TARGETING HOMEWORK 2 © PASCAL PRESS ISBN 9781925726442

② The animals that made nests in the old man's beard are all

☐ **a** birds. ☐ **c** fish.

☐ **b** amphibians. ☐ **d** mammals.

③ How many animals had made nests in the old man's beard?

☐ **a** 2 ☐ **c** 4

☐ **b** 6 ☐ **d** 8

④ Which birds were there most of?

☐ **a** owls ☐ **c** hens

☐ **b** larks ☐ **d** wrens

⑤ Which words best describe the old man's beard?

☐ **a** short and clipped

☐ **b** long and neat

☐ **c** untamed and scruffy

☐ **d** neatly trimmed

⑥ Find a word in the poem that rhymes with **beard**.

_____

⑦ Find a word in the poem that rhymes with **hen**.

_____

⑧ How do you think the old man felt about having animals in his beard.

☐ **a** surprised ☐ **c** proud

☐ **b** excited ☐ **d** disgusted

⑨ This poem is called a nonsense poem. Why?

☐ **a** It is silly.

☐ **b** It only has two rhymes.

☐ **c** It's too short to be a real poem.

☐ **d** The poet doesn't like long beards.

⑩ Why do you think the poet wrote this poem?

☐ **a** to teach people about beards

☐ **b** to warn people that birds can make nests in beards.

☐ **c** to make us laugh

☐ **d** to tell people to not grow beards

TERM 1 ENGLISH

Score 2 points for each correct answer!

SCORE **/20** (0-8) (10-14) (16-20)

My Book Review

Title _____

Author _____

Colour stars to show your rating. ☆ ☆ ☆ ☆ ☆
Boring   Great!

Comment _____

_____

Counting in 10s

① Count in 10s. Write the numbers you count.

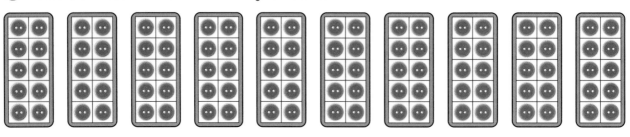

_____ _____ _____ _____ _____ _____ _____ _____ _____ _____

TERM 1 MATHS

② Use green to colour the numbers you counted above on the 100 grid.

③ Use blue to colour number **7**. Add on 10. Colour it blue too.

Continue adding 10 and colouring the numbers blue.

④ Write the numbers you coloured.

_____, _____, _____, _____, _____,

_____, _____, _____, _____, _____,

1	2	3	4	5	6	7	8	9	10
11	12	13	14	15	16	17	18	19	20
21	22	23	24	25	26	27	28	29	30
31	32	33	34	35	36	37	38	39	40
41	42	43	44	45	46	47	48	49	50
51	52	53	54	55	56	57	58	59	60
61	62	63	64	65	66	67	68	69	70
71	72	73	74	75	76	77	78	79	80
81	82	83	84	85	86	87	88	89	90
91	92	93	94	95	96	97	98	99	100

⑤ Use yellow to colour number **5**. Add on 10. Colour it yellow too.

Continue adding 10 and colouring the numbers yellow.

⑥ Write the numbers you coloured.

_____, _____, _____, _____, _____, _____, _____, _____, _____, _____

⑦ Use pink to colour number **2**. Add on 10. Colour it pink too.
Continue adding 10 and colouring the numbers pink.

⑧ Write the numbers you coloured.

_____, _____, _____, _____, _____, _____, _____, _____, _____, _____

⑨ Use orange to colour number **8**. Add on 10. Colour it orange too.
Continue adding 10 and colouring the numbers orange.

⑩ Write the numbers you coloured.

_____, _____, _____, _____, _____, _____, _____, _____, _____, _____

Now you can count in tens, starting from any number!

TARGETING HOMEWORK 2 © PASCAL PRESS ISBN 9781925726442

Write the total number of blocks. Remember to count in tens and then add the ones.

⑪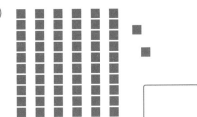

⑫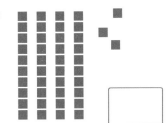

⑬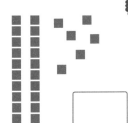

⑭ Colour some of these sheep blue. Colour the other sheep yellow.

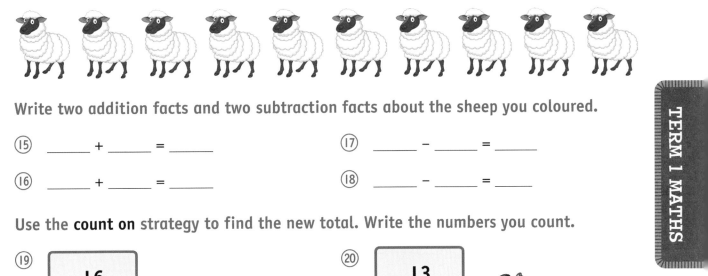

Write two addition facts and two subtraction facts about the sheep you coloured.

⑮ _____ + _____ = _____

⑯ _____ + _____ = _____

⑰ _____ – _____ = _____

⑱ _____ – _____ = _____

Use the **count on** strategy to find the new total. Write the numbers you count.

⑲ | 16 |

_____, _____, _____

⑳ | 13 |

_____, _____

Write the **doubles addition facts** shown on these dice.

㉑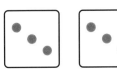

_____ + _____ = _____

㉒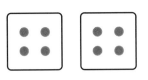

_____ + _____ = _____

㉓

_____ + _____ = _____

㉔

_____ + _____ = _____

Read the word problems.
Write the addition or subtraction fact you use to work out the answer.

㉕ The farmer had 10 sheep in one paddock and 4 sheep in another paddock.
How many sheep did she have altogether?

_____

TERM 1 MATHS

Number & Algebra

TERM 1 MATHS

㉖ There were 12 puppies in the pet shop.
Three puppies were sold.
How many puppies are left in the pet shop? _____

㉗ Write a word problem for this addition fact: **5 + 3 = 8**

_____

_____

Fractions – half

Tick the shapes that are divided in half. Cross the shapes that are not in halves.

㉘   ㉚  ㉜

㉙  ㉛    ㉝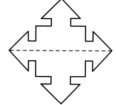

Draw lines to divide these shapes in half. How many different ways can you find?

㉞  ㉟  ㊱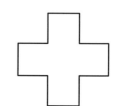

Sam and Jamie shared the toys so that they got half each.
Use blue to circle Sam's half and use orange to circle Jamie's half.

㊲

㊳

㊴

Score 2 points for each correct answer! SCORE /78 0–36 38–72 74–78

32

TARGETING HOMEWORK 2 © PASCAL PRESS ISBN 9781925726442

Collecting data

Sarah asked her friends to tell their favourite ice-cream flavour. She wrote their choices on a chart.

Sam	vanilla
Zayne	mango
Hana	chocolate
Sasha	chocolate
Tema	chocolate
Mosi	strawberry
Jamie	choc–mint
Ari	chocolate
Nala	vanilla
Li	chocolate
Ali	mango
Tan	mango

① List the flavours of ice cream that Sarah's friends liked. Use tally marks to show how many votes each flavour received.

_____

_____

_____

_____

_____

② Write the question Sarah would have asked her friends.

_____

③ Write a statement that tells what Sarah found out.

_____

_____

Score 2 points for each correct answer! SCORE /6

TERM 1 MATHS

Problem Solving

AC9M2N03

Sam had a bag of 16 marbles. He shared them with Nala so they had half each.

Mosi wanted some marbles too. Sam shared the marbles he had left with Mosi, so they had half each.

When Zayne came to play, he wanted some marbles too. Sam shared the marbles he had left with Zayne, so they had half each.

① How many marbles did Sam give Zayne?

_____

② Who had the most marbles?

_____

Draw a picture here to help you solve this problem.

Grammar & Punctuation

Read the groups of words. Write S if it is a sentence.
Draw a cross if it is not a sentence.

① _____ the little yellow duck

② _____ The little yellow duck swam in the pond.

③ _____ I came first in the race.

④ _____ The dog chased the ball across the park.

⑤ _____ at the beach

Read this sentence: Our team won the soccer match on Friday.

Write questions about this sentence. Put a question mark at the end of each one.

⑥ Who _____

⑦ What _____

⑧ When _____

Read these sentences. Write R if the sentence is a request. Write C if it is a command.

⑨ _____ Put your book on the table.

⑩ _____ May I have an icecream, please?

⑪ _____ Will you close the door, please?

⑫ _____ Come to the table now.

Add the missing commas.

⑬ I packed my shirts shorts socks underwear and pyjamas into my bag.

⑭ Sam invited Sarah Zayne Tema and Jake to his birthday party.

⑮ At the farm, Sam saw horses cows sheep goats and dogs.

Circle the verb in each sentence.

⑯ The cat ate the food hungrily.

⑰ The birds sang from the treetops.

⑱ The children wrote stories in their books.

⑲ The waves washed the sandcastle into the sea.

⑳ The turtles laid their eggs on the sand.

Score 2 points for each correct answer! **SCORE** **/40** (0-18) (20-34) (36-40)

TARGETING HOMEWORK 2 © PASCAL PRESS ISBN 9781925726442

Phonic Knowledge & Spelling

Write the word and its correct ending – ing or ed – to finish the sentences.

① **look** The children were _____ at the horses in the paddock.

② **bake** My brother _____ a cake for the school fete.

③ **tip** The toddler _____ all the toys onto the floor.

④ **wave** The children were _____ goodbye from the train.

⑤ **wash** The women _____ the dog under the hose.

Cross out the incorrect word in each sentence.

⑥ The superhero's **cap cape** flapped behind her when she flew through the sky.

⑦ Everyone thought the little lion **cub cube** was very cute.

⑧ The teacher told the children to **hop hope** on one foot.

⑨ The children watched the **kit kite** fly high in the sky.

Circle the word that has a different vowel sound.

⑩ eight snail main apple

⑪ rid kite try might

⑫ dune music us few

⑬ meet grey seat bead

⑭ boat note top grow

Choose words from the box to complete these sentences.

⑮ The lions were given big pieces of _____ to eat.

⑯ The band was learning a new piece of _____ for the concert.

⑰ The horse's _____ was braided for the show.

⑱ The children were tired when they got _____.

⑲ The girl rolled a piece of paper to make a _____.

⑳ The family liked to _____ board games on the weekend.

㉑ The baker put some orange _____ into the carrot cake.

㉒ The boy ran so fast he got a stitch in his _____.

㉓ The boy got blisters on his feet because his shoes were too _____.

| home |
| meat |
| music |
| peel |
| play |
| side |
| tail |
| tight |
| tube |

Score 2 points for each correct answer! SCORE **/46**   0-20   22-40   42-46

TERM 1 MATHS

Write the missing numbers.
Circle **F** if you are counting **forwards**. Circle **B** if you are counting **backwards**.
Then circle the number to tell how you are counting.

①
| 62 | 64 | | | | 72 | | | | 80 |

I am counting F B in 1s 2s 5s 10s

②
| 50 | | 60 | | | | | 85 | | |

I am counting F B in 1s 2s 5s 10s

③
| 100 | 90 | 80 | | | | | | 20 | |

I am counting F B in 1s 2s 5s 10s

④
| 38 | | | 41 | | 43 | | | | |

I am counting F B in 1s 2s 5s 10s

⑤
| 7 | | 27 | 37 | | | | | 87 | |

I am counting F B in 1s 2s 5s 10s

⑥
| 78 | 76 | | | 70 | | | | | 60 |

I am counting F B in 1s 2s 5s 10s

⑦ Circle the numbers that are **more than 50**:   76   36   52   89   19

⑧ Circle the numbers that are **less than 50**:   85   25   36   63   15

Write how many blocks altogether.

⑨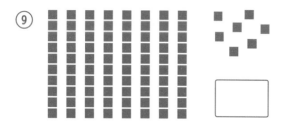

⑩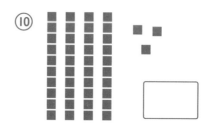

TARGETING HOMEWORK 2 © PASCAL PRESS ISBN 9781925726442

Write two addition facts and two subtraction facts for each of these dominoes.

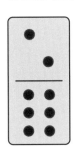

⑪ _____ + _____ = _____

⑫ _____ + _____ = _____

⑬ _____ – _____ = _____

⑭ _____ – _____ = _____

⑮ _____ + _____ = _____

⑯ _____ + _____ = _____

⑰ _____ – _____ = _____

⑱ _____ – _____ = _____

Write the value of these coins.

⑲ _____

⑳ _____

㉑ _____

Score 2 points for each correct answer! SCORE /42 0-18 20-36 38-42

TERM 1 MATHS

Measurement & Space

Look at these shapes.

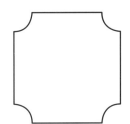

① Use blue to colour the shape that has only curved sides.

② Use yellow to colour the shape that has only straight sides.

③ Use green to colour the shape that has curved sides and straight sides.

Write the time shown on these clocks.

④

⑤

⑥

⑦

_____   _____   _____   _____

Score 2 points for each correct answer! SCORE /14 0-4 6-10 12-14

TARGETING HOMEWORK 2 © PASCAL PRESS ISBN 9781925726442

37

Grammar & Punctuation

AC9E2LA07

TERM 2 ENGLISH

Common nouns

Common nouns are the names of people, places and things. For example: boy, girl, man, woman, dog, cat, horse, cow, hill, town, city, river, apple, watch, hammer.

Circle the common nouns in these sentences.

① A girl sat on a seat under a tree.

② A dog chewed on a bone behind the house.

③ A bird pulled a worm out of the ground.

④ A kangaroo jumped the fence to eat the grass in the paddock.

Adjectives

Adjectives describe or add more information to nouns. For example: beautiful, big, clever, kind, red, hard, rough, funny, high, empty, long, happy, open, expensive.

Circle the adjectives in these sentences.

⑤ A little girl sat on a wooden seat under a shady tree.

⑥ A hungry dog chewed on a dry bone behind the old house.

⑦ A brown bird pulled a long worm out of the wet ground.

⑧ A big kangaroo jumped the high fence to eat the long grass in the green paddock.

Circle one adjective to describe the noun. Then use the adjective and noun in a sentence.

⑨ **apple**   crunchy   red   wrinkly   bad

_____

⑩ **road**   dirt   long   bumpy   city

_____

Write a word that means the opposite of these adjectives.

⑪ happy _____   ⑭ long _____

⑫ empty _____   ⑮ open _____

⑬ heavy _____

Score 2 points for each correct answer!   SCORE **/30**   (0-12)   (14-24)   (26-30)

Phonic Knowledge & Spelling

Long vowel sounds – i, e, o, ow, oo

Read the words in these lists. The words in each list have the same vowel sound.

long i as in pie	long e as in baby	long o as in toe	long ow as in cow	long oo as in zoo
die	cutie	doe	now	do
lie	cozy	oboe	down	too
tie	eerie	blow	frown	moo
cry	movie	flow	how	moon
fly	oldie	glow	towel	pool
try	baddie	throw	bow	hoop
shy	happy	low	brown	blue
by	pony	show	gown	glue
my	sunny	tow	pow	true
fry	lady	bow	wow	shoe

Choose words from the lists to complete these sentences.

① The baby bird was learning to _____.

② We watched a funny _____ last night.

③ My big _____ hurt when I kicked it on a stone.

④ The farmer milked the _____ every morning before dawn.

⑤ The astronaut was ready for her trip to the _____.

⑥ Cinderella wore a beautiful _____ to the ball.

⑦ The children were hoping for a _____ day after all the rain.

⑧ My father taught me how to _____ up a balloon.

⑨ The paper didn't stick because I didn't use enough _____.

⑩ The _____ was too tight for my foot and I got a blister.

Circle the word that has a different vowel sound.

⑪ fly cry lady tie

⑫ glow brown show doe

⑬ down blow frown now

⑭ happy movie pie cutie

⑮ zoo blue moon shook

Score 2 points for each correct answer! **SCORE** **/30** (0-12) (14-24) (26-30)

Imaginative text – Narrative

The Not So Empty Tent

One day, the Circus Bizurkus troupe went out for a walk.

They saw an old circus tent. They thought they heard voices coming from it, so they went inside.

Inside the tent, there were monsters.

When they saw the monsters, they were too surprised to make a sound.

When the monsters saw the circus troupe, they were so shocked they just stared.

The biggest monster said, "Who are you?"

"We are the Circus Bizurkus," said Ringmaster Roy.

"What is a circus?" asked the monster with five eyes.

"You live in a circus tent, but you don't know what a circus is?" asked Bendy Betty.

"The tent was empty, so we moved in," said the monster with twelve arms.

"Let us show you what a circus can be!" cried Ringmaster Roy.

The circus troupe performed their tricks.

"We want to be a circus troupe too!" the monsters cried.

Source: Storylands Circus Bizurkus, *The Not So Empty Tent*, Blake Education

Write or tick the correct answer.

① What did the circus troupe hear coming from the old circus tent?

☐ **a** singing ☐ **b** music ☐ **c** voices ☐ **d** laughter

TARGETING HOMEWORK 2 © PASCAL PRESS ISBN 9781925726442

② What was inside the tent?

☐ **a** a musical band ☐ **c** a circus

☐ **b** monsters ☐ **d** nothing

③ How did Circus Bizurkus feel when they saw the monsters?

_____

④ What did Circus Bizurkus do when they saw the monsters?

☐ **a** They ran away.

☐ **b** They screamed.

☐ **c** They didn't make a sound.

☐ **d** They stared.

⑤ How did the monsters feel when Circus Bizurkus came into the tent?

_____

⑥ What did the monster do when Circus Bizurkus came into the tent?

☐ **a** They ran away.

☐ **b** They screamed.

☐ **c** They didn't make a sound.

☐ **d** They stared.

⑦ Why were the monsters living in the tent?

☐ **a** They were on holiday.

☐ **b** It was empty, so they moved in.

☐ **c** They were pretending to be a circus.

☐ **d** They wanted to scare people.

⑧ How did the monsters feel when Circus Bizurkus performed their tricks?

☐ **a** scared ☐ **c** shocked

☐ **b** excited ☐ **d** worried

⑨ What did the monsters say after Circus Bizurkus performed their tricks?

☐ **a** We can do better than that.

☐ **b** We want to be a circus troupe too!

☐ **c** Circus tricks are not very exciting.

☐ **d** Now we are going to eat you.

⑩ Do you think Circus Bizurkus will let the monsters join their circus?

☐ **a** Yes ☐ **b** No

TERM 2 ENGLISH

Score 2 points for each correct answer!

SCORE /20 (0-8) (10-14) (16-20)

My Book Review

Title _____

Author _____

Colour stars to show your rating: ☆ ☆ ☆ ☆ ☆

Boring   Great!

Comment _____

_____

UNIT 10

Number & Algebra

AC9M2N01, AC9M2N02, AC9M2N05, AC9M2N06, AC9M2A01, AC9M2A03

Numbers over 100

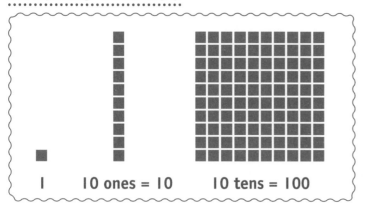

| | 10 ones = 10 | 10 tens = 100 |

① Count in **ones**. Write the numbers you count.

____, ____, ____, ____, ____, ____, ____, ____, ____, ____

② Count in **tens**. Write the numbers you count.

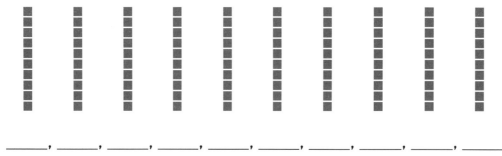

_____, _____, _____, _____, _____, _____, _____, _____, _____, _____

③ Count in **hundreds**. Write the numbers you count.

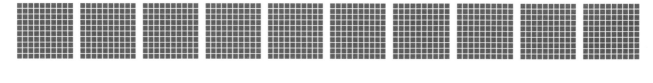

_____ _____ _____ _____ _____ _____ _____ _____ _____ _____

Write the missing numbers.

④ 7, 17, 27, _____, _____, _____, 67, _____, _____, _____

⑤ 107, 117, 127, _____, _____, _____, 167, _____, _____, _____

⑥ 5, 10, 15, _____, _____, _____, 35, _____, _____, _____

⑦ 105, 110, 115, _____, _____, _____, 135, _____, _____, _____

⑧ 220, 230, 240, _____, _____, _____, 280, _____, _____, _____

TARGETING HOMEWORK 2 © PASCAL PRESS ISBN 9781925726442

Write how many.

⑨

⑩

⑪

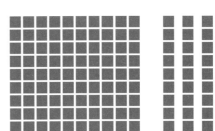

Draw blocks to show these numbers.

⑫ 7

⑬ 27

⑭ 127

Write the numbers shown on these abacuses.

⑮

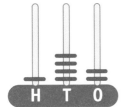

____ hundred, ____ tens, ____ ones

= _____

⑯

____ hundreds, ____ ten, ____ ones

= _____

Use your knowledge of the hundreds chart to fill in the numbers on the puzzle pieces.

⑰

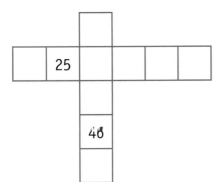

25

46

⑱

52

72

Number & Algebra

⑲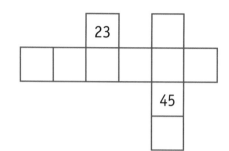

23

45

⑳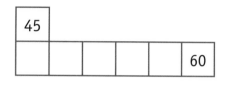

45

60

These hoops and balls are set out for the sports lesson.

㉑ How many hoops are there? _____

㉒ How many balls are there in each hoop? _____

㉓ 2 hoops with 5 balls each makes _____ balls altogether.

㉔ 2 lots of 5 = _____

Score 2 points for each correct answer!

SCORE **/48** (0-22) (24-42) (44-48)

Measurement & Space

AC9M2SP01

2D shapes

Know your shapes.

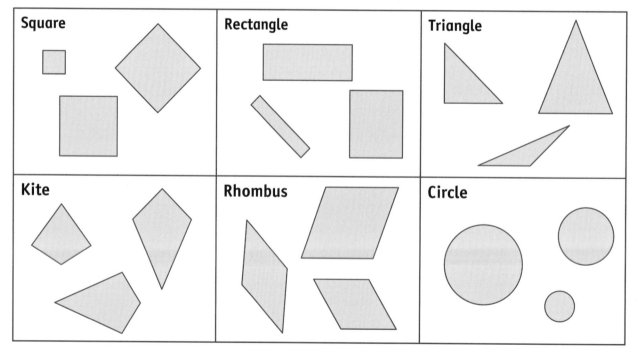

TARGETING HOMEWORK 2 © PASCAL PRESS ISBN 9781925726442

① Which five shapes have straight sides?

_____

_____

② Which shape has curved sides?

_____

③ Which shape has 3 straight sides?

_____

④ Which two shapes have 4 straight sides that are all the same length?

_____

⑤ Which two shapes have 2 long straight sides and 2 shorter straight sides?

_____

⑥ How many corners does a square have? _____

⑦ How many corners does a triangle have? _____

⑧ How many corners does a circle have? _____

⑨ How many corners does a kite have? _____

⑩ How many corners does a rhombus have? _____

Score 2 points for each correct answer! | SCORE | /20 (0-8) (10-14) (16-20)

TERM 2 MATHS

Problem Solving

AC9M2SP01

How many triangles can you find?

Trace the outline of the triangles in different colours.

Hint: There are more than 20.

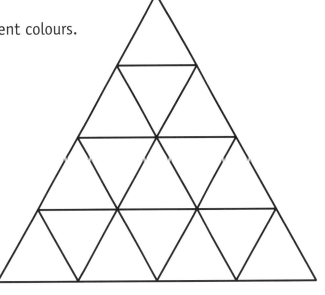

Grammar & Punctuation

AC9E2LA07

Abstract nouns

Common nouns are the names of people, places and things.
Abstract nouns are the names of **ideas** and **feelings**. They are things you can't see or touch. For example: dream, happiness, loneliness, memory, friendship, joy, fear, thought.

Circle the abstract nouns in these sentences.

① The thought of going to the moon is very exciting.

② The elderly woman had a memory of her first flight overseas when she was a child.

③ The boy said he didn't have a reason for taking the marble.

④ The girls did everything together because they had a close friendship.

⑤ The children were learning to control their anger by calming down with meditation.

⑥ Last night I had a dream about being able to fly.

Write C for common nouns. Write A for abstract nouns.

⑦ _____ hair

⑧ _____ thoughtfulness

⑨ _____ forgiveness

⑩ _____ pet

⑪ _____ happiness

⑫ _____ boat

⑬ _____ reason

⑭ _____ comb

⑮ _____ idea

Adverbs

Adverbs tell you more about a **verb** (an action or doing word). **Adverbs** often end with **ly**. For example: quickly, slowly, happily, sadly, easily, badly, carefully, thoughtfully, secretly, busily.

Circle the verb in each sentence.
Then choose an adverb from the list above to complete the sentence.

⑯ The dog ran home _____.

⑰ The girl whispered _____ to her friends.

⑱ The children completed their work _____.

⑲ The tired old man walked _____ down the road.

⑳ The boy danced _____ around the garden.

Score 2 points for each correct answer! **SCORE** **/40** (0-18) (20-34) (36-40)

TARGETING HOMEWORK 2 © PASCAL PRESS ISBN 9781925726442

Long vowel sounds – ou, oy, oi, au

Read the words in these lists. The words in each list have the **same vowel sound.**

long ou as in **house**	long oy as in **boy**	long oi as in **coin**	long au as in **sauce**
mouse	toy	join	August
round	coy	point	because
about	annoy	soil	taught
found	soy	boil	audio
cloud	joy	spoil	astronaut
loud	oyster	toilet	autumn
south	royal	oink	launch
mouth	loyal	voice	author
sprout	enjoy	coil	cause
proud	destroy	oil	pause

TERM 2 ENGLISH

Choose words from the lists to complete these sentences.

① The _____ was in the rocket, ready to go to the moon.

② The toddler played with the _____ in the waiting room.

③ There was just one little white _____ in the sky.

④ The children planted the seeds in the _____.

⑤ The monster threatened to _____ the city.

⑥ The boy was told to take the pencil out of his _____.

⑦ The _____ noise woke the baby.

⑧ The girl had to speak in a loud _____ so she could be heard.

⑨ The police investigated the _____ of the crash.

⑩ The boy asked if he could _____ in the game.

Circle the word that has a different vowel sound.

⑪ mouse   cloud   you   mouth

⑫ August   aunt   autumn   cause

⑬ voice   destroy   annoy   about

⑭ toy   toil   joy   toll

⑮ oink   loud   found   about

Score 2 points
for each
correct answer!

SCORE **/30** 0-12 14-24 26-30

TERM 2 ENGLISH

What Do Animals Eat?

Some animals are **carnivores**. They eat meat.

Some animals are **herbivores**. They eat plants.

Some animals are **omnivores**.

They eat meat and plants.

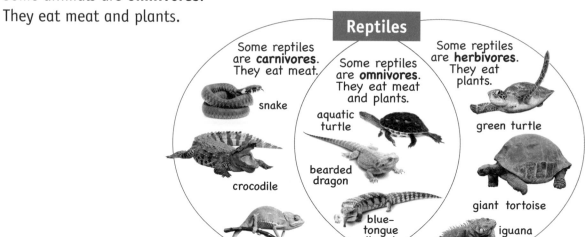

Reptiles

Some reptiles are **carnivores**. They eat meat.
snake
crocodile
chameleon

Some reptiles are **omnivores**. They eat meat and plants.
aquatic turtle
bearded dragon
blue-tongue lizard

Some reptiles are **herbivores**. They eat plants.
green turtle
giant tortoise
iguana

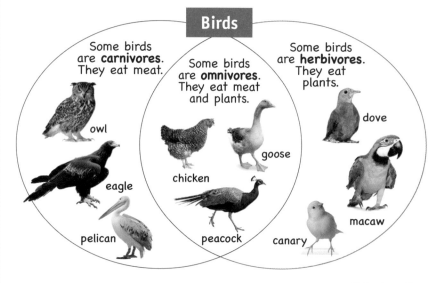

Birds

Some birds are **carnivores**. They eat meat.
owl
eagle
pelican

Some birds are **omnivores**. They eat meat and plants.
chicken
goose
peacock

Some birds are **herbivores**. They eat plants.
dove
macaw
canary

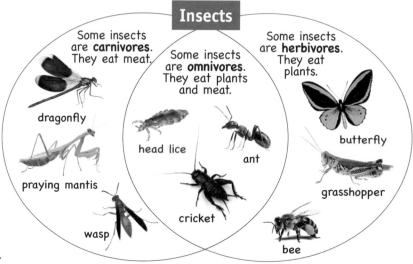

Insects

Some insects are **carnivores**. They eat meat.
dragonfly
praying mantis
wasp

Some insects are **omnivores**. They eat plants and meat.
head lice
ant
cricket

Some insects are **herbivores**. They eat plants.
butterfly
grasshopper
bee

Source: Steve Parish First Facts, *Birds*, *Reptiles*, and *Insects*, Pascal Press

Write or tick the correct answer.

① Which insects are **carnivores**?

☐ a crickets   ☐ c butterflies

☐ b wasps   ☐ d bees

② Which birds are **carnivores**?

☐ a geese   ☐ c macaws

☐ b peacocks   ☐ d pelicans

③ Which reptiles are **herbivores**?

☐ a chameleons

☐ b bearded dragons

☐ c iguanas

☐ d crocodiles

④ Which animals eat only plants?

☐ a herbivores   ☐ c omnivores

☐ b carnivores   ☐ d insects

⑤ Which insects are **omnivores**?

☐ a butterflies

☐ b praying mantises

☐ c ants

☐ d bees

⑥ Which animals eat only plants?

☐ a tortoises   ☐ c peacocks

☐ b chameleons   ☐ d crickets

⑦ Which reptiles are **omnivores**?

☐ a bearded dragons

☐ b chameleons

☐ c snakes

☐ d iguanas

⑧ What do canaries eat?

☐ a plants

☐ b meat

☐ c plants and meat

⑨ Which animal group do macaws belong to?

☐ a insects   ☐ c birds

☐ b reptiles   ☐ d other

⑩ Which animal is not a **reptile**?

☐ a tortoise   ☐ c iguana

☐ b snake   ☐ d cricket

TERM 2 ENGLISH

Score 2 points for each correct answer!   SCORE   **/ 20**   (0-8)   (10-14)   (16-20)

My Book Review

Title _____

Author _____

Colour stars to show your rating: ☆ ☆ ☆ ☆ ☆

                              Boring   Great!

Comment _____

_____

Numbers over 100

TERM 2 MATHS

① Start with **1**. Add on **10**. Keep adding **10**. Write the numbers you count.

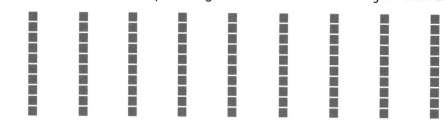

_____, _____, _____, _____, _____, _____, _____, _____, _____, _____

② Start with **1**. Add on **100**. Keep adding **100**. Write the numbers you count.

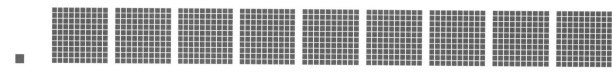

_____ _____ _____ _____ _____ _____ _____ _____ _____ _____

③ Start with **10**. Add on **100**. Keep adding **100**. Write the numbers you count.

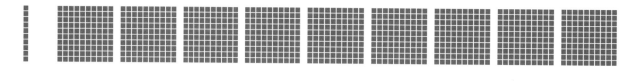

_____ _____ _____ _____ _____ _____ _____ _____ _____ _____

Continue these counting patterns.

④ 100, 101, 102, 103, _____, _____, _____, _____, _____.

⑤ 100, 102, 104, 106, _____, _____, _____, _____, _____.

⑥ 100, 105, 110, 115, _____, _____, _____, _____, _____.

⑦ 100, 110, 120, 130, _____, _____, _____, _____, _____.

⑧ 320, 321, 322, 323, _____, _____, _____, _____, _____.

⑨ 520, 522, 524, 526, _____, _____, _____, _____, _____.

⑩ 103, 203, 303, 403, _____, _____, _____, _____, _____.

Write how many you see.

⑪

⑫

TARGETING HOMEWORK 2 © PASCAL PRESS ISBN 9781925726442

Circle the largest number.

⑬   327   742   273   568   801

⑭   862   102   347   921   435

⑮   Draw 3 apples on each plate.

⑯   How many plates are there? ____

⑰   How many apples on each plate? ____

⑱   How many apples altogether? ____

⑲   3 + 3 = ____

⑳   2 groups of 3 = ____

㉗   Draw 3 fish in each bowl.

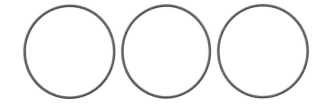

㉘   How many bowls are there? ____

㉙   How many fish in each bowl? ____

㉚   How many fish altogether? ____

㉛   3 + 3 + 3 = ____

㉜   3 groups of 3 = ____

㉑   Draw 4 sheep in each pen.

㉒   How many pens are there? ____

㉓   How many sheep in each pen? ____

㉔   How many sheep altogether? ____

㉕   4 + 4 = ____

㉖   2 groups of 4 = ____

㉝   Draw 2 balls in each hoop.

㉞   How many hoops are there? ____

㉟   How many balls in each hoop? ____

㊱   How many balls altogether? ____

㊲   2 + 2 + 2 = ____

㊳   3 groups of 2 = ____

㊴   Draw a picture to show 4 groups of 2. Write how many altogether.

TARGETING HOMEWORK 2 © PASCAL PRESS ISBN 9781925726442

Score 2 points for each correct answer!   SCORE   **/78**   (0-36)   (38-72)   (74-78)

UNIT **12**

TERM 2 MATHS

Location and transformation – placing objects on a map

Look at this map. Sam's house is located at **G1**. Zane's house is located at **B9**.

	A	B	C	D	E	F	G	H	I
9		Zane							
8									
7									
6									
5									
4									
3									
2									
1							Sam		

TERM 2 MATHS

When Sam visits Zane, he passes these landmarks.
Draw pictures to show their location on the map.

① F2: tree

② A9: icecream shop

③ D4: Post Office

④ H3: swing

⑤ B7: flower garden

⑥ E6: house with a barking dog

⑦ F4: fountain

⑧ B6, C6: School

⑦ F4: fountain

⑧ B6, C6: School

⑨ **Draw a line on the road to show how Sam gets to Zane's house.**

⑩ Write the directions, including the turns.

_____

_____

_____

_____

_____

TARGETING HOMEWORK 2 © PASCAL PRESS ISBN 9781925726442

Time – half hours and quarter hours

When the **big hand** points straight down to **6**, it has travelled **halfway** around the clock from 12. It is **half past** the hour.

When the **big hand** points to **3**, it has travelled only a **quarter** of the way around the clock from 12. It is a **quarter past** the hour. The **little hand** has moved just one quarter of the way past the hour.

half past 2

quarter past 2

These clocks all show **quarter past the hour.** Complete the time.

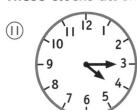

⑪ quarter past ____   ⑫ quarter past ____   ⑬ quarter past ____   ⑭ quarter past ____

Draw the missing hand to show the time.

⑮ quarter past 6   ⑯ quarter past 2   ⑰ quarter past 9   ⑱ quarter past 5

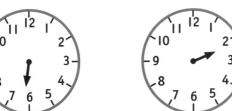  

Draw the hands to show the time.

⑲ quarter past 1

⑳ quarter past 7

Score 2 points for each correct answer!

SCORE **/40** 0-18 20-34 36-40

Problem Solving

AC9M2N01

Number Riddles – What number am I? Circle the correct answer in the box.

① | 45 35 25 30 43 37 40 50 |

Clues: I am more than 30.
I am less than 40.
You count me when you count in 5s.

② | 15 17 51 71 16 61 18 81 |

Clues: I am a teen number.
I am more than 15.
I am less than 17.

Grammar & Punctuation

AC9E2LA07, AC9E2LA10, AC9E2LY12

Proper nouns

> **Proper nouns** are the names of specific people, places and things.
> A **proper noun** begins with a **capital letter**.
> For example: Zayne, Miss Davis, Australia, Colo River, Sydney Opera House, Rudd Street.

Circle the proper nouns in these sentences.

① The name of my teacher is Ms Pan.

② The children named their kitten Rex.

③ On Saturday, we will go to the beach.

④ I saw Tema at the football last night.

⑤ The Gold Coast is in Queensland.

⑥ Canberra is the capital of Australia.

Using capital letters for titles

> **Capital letters** are used for the most important words in titles, including the titles of books, stories, poems, movies and video games. We also put these titles in *italics*.
> For example: *The Lost Dog*, *Goldilocks and the Three Bears*.

Underline the main words in each title and then write the title correctly.

⑦ little red riding hood _____

⑧ the butterfly and the bee _____

⑨ snakes and lizards _____

Making nouns from verbs

> We can add an **ending** to a **verb** to make a **noun** that means 'one who ...'
> For example, add **er** to the verb **paint**, and you get the noun **painter**, which means 'one who paints'. A **writer** is one who writes. We usually add **er** to verbs with one syllable.

Add er to the end of these verbs to make a noun. Explain the meaning.

	Verb	Noun (add er)	Meaning
⑩	teach	_____	one who _____
⑪	drive	_____	one who _____
⑫	learn	_____	one who _____
⑬	bake	_____	one who _____
⑭	speak	_____	one who _____

Score 2 points for each correct answer!

SCORE **/28**

TERM 2 ENGLISH

Phonic Knowledge & Spelling

AC9E2LY08, AC9E2LY10, AC9E2LY11

Long vowel sounds – ar, er, ir, ur, or

Read the words in these lists. The words in each list have the same vowel sound.

long ar as in car	long er as in her	long ir as in bird	long ur as in hurt	long or as in fork
far	were	fir	nurse	cork
shark	fern	first	burn	more
card	herd	thirsty	turtle	saw
jar	germ	birthday	curl	war
star	stern	girl	fur	sure
craft	person	shirt	Thursday	door
half	mermaid	stir	surf	port
calf	tiger	circle	Saturday	torch
palm	letter	dirt	surprise	sport
giraffe	water	chirp	burp	board

Choose words from the lists to complete these sentences.

① The boy wore a _____ that had a picture of a shark on it.

② The children helped feed the baby _____ with a bottle of milk.

③ The family watched the _____ lay its eggs in the sand.

④ The _____ on the old house swung open when the wind blew.

⑤ The mermaid swam in the warm sea _____.

⑥ Jake wrote a _____ to his grandmother on the weekend.

⑦ We are going to the beach on _____.

⑧ The children shone the light from the _____ onto the possum.

⑨ The family chose the tallest _____ tree to be their Christmas tree.

⑩ Every Friday afternoon, the children did _____ at school.

Circle the word that has a different vowel sound.

⑪ shark chirp surf fern

⑫ burp dirt germ torch

⑬ were war thirsty burn

⑭ board calf jar giraffe

⑮ door saw first sure

Score 2 points for each correct answer!

SCORE **/30** 0-12 14-24 26-30

TERM 2 ENGLISH

Trace the words. Start at the star. Follow the arrows.

The girl had a
surprise birthday
party yesterday.

TERM 2 ENGLISH

Reading & Comprehension

Informative text – Procedure

AC9E2LA03, AC9E2LA08, AC9E2LY03, AC9E2LY05

How to Make Fruit Skewers

You need:
- a variety of fruit
- a knife
- skewers

What to do:
1 Wash the fruit.
2 Peel the fruit, if necessary.
3 Cut the fruit into bite-sized pieces.
4 Thread pieces of fruit onto the skewers.
5 Serve and enjoy!

Write or tick the correct answer.

① This text is a
- ☐ **a** poem.
- ☐ **b** persuasive text.
- ☐ **c** story.
- ☐ **d** recipe.

② This text explains how to
- ☐ **a** peel fruit.
- ☐ **b** make fruit skewers.
- ☐ **c** make fruit salad.
- ☐ **d** grow fruit and berries.

③ The first thing you need to do is

☐ **a** wash the fruit.

☐ **b** thread the fruit onto the skewers.

☐ **c** eat the fruit.

☐ **d** peel the fruit.

④ Which of these does the recipe **not** tell you to do?

☐ **a** Grow the fruit.

☐ **b** Wash the fruit.

☐ **c** Cut the fruit.

☐ **d** Thread the fruit onto skewers.

⑤ Which fruits would you put onto skewers? List three.

_____

_____

_____

⑥ What size does the fruit need to be?

_____

⑦ Which of the following would you **not** put on a fruit skewer?

☐ **a** strawberries   ☐ **c** apples

☐ **b** carrot   ☐ **d** banana

⑧ Are fruit skewers a healthy treat or an unhealthy treat?

☐ **a** healthy

☐ **b** unhealthy

⑨ Which fruit would you **not** need to cut to put on skewers?

☐ **a** kiwi fruit   ☐ **c** grapes

☐ **b** apples   ☐ **d** oranges

⑩ Which of these fruits would you need to cut to put on skewers?

☐ **a** watermelon

☐ **b** strawberries

☐ **c** raspberries

☐ **d** blueberries

TERM 2 ENGLISH

Score 2 points for each correct answer!

SCORE | **/20** | 0-8 | 10-14 | 16-20

My Book Review

Title _____

Author _____

Colour stars to show your rating: ☆ ☆ ☆ ☆ ☆

Boring   Great!

Comment _____

_____

Numbers over 100

Write the missing numbers in these sequences.

① 210, 211, 212, _____, _____, _____, _____, 217, _____, _____

② 375, 374, 373, _____, _____, _____, 369, 368, _____, _____

③ 25, 30, 35, 40, _____, _____, _____, _____, 65, _____, _____

④ 42, 44, 46, 48, _____, _____, _____, _____, _____, _____, 62

⑤ 87, 187, 287, 387, _____, _____, _____, _____, 887, _____

Write how many hundreds, tens and ones you see. Write how many altogether.

⑥ _____ hundreds + _____ tens + _____ ones = ☐

⑦ _____ hundreds + _____ tens + _____ ones = ☐

Look at these numbers on the abacus. Draw blocks to show the number. Write how many hundreds, tens and ones. Write how many altogether.

⑧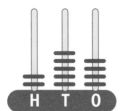

_____ hundreds, _____ tens, _____ ones

= _____

⑨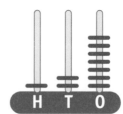

_____ hundred, _____ tens, _____ ones

= _____

Circle the largest number.

⑩ 134 276 843 715 865

⑪ 578 95 410 800 563

Circle the smallest number.

⑫ 473 167 918 329 500

⑬ 480 218 936 224 73

TERM 2 MATHS

Doubles

Sometimes when you play a game, you have to roll a double to start.
Double means **two the same.** Draw dots on these dice to show the doubles.

⑭ **Double 1**

2 ones

= _____ altogether

⑰ **Double 4**

2 fours

= _____ altogether

⑮ **Double 2**

2 twos

= _____ altogether

⑱ **Double 5**

2 fives

= _____ altogether

⑯ **Double 3**

2 threes

= _____ altogether

⑲ **Double 6**

2 sixes

= _____ altogether

Draw dots in each of these rows to show doubles. Then write how many altogether.

⑳ **Double 7**

2 sevens = _____ altogether

㉒ **Double 9**

2 nines = _____ altogether

㉑ **Double 8**

2 eights = _____ altogether

㉓ **Double 10**

2 tens = _____ altogether

Money

We use these bank notes for larger amounts of money.

㉔ What colour is the note that has greatest value? _____

㉕ What colour is the note that has smallest value? _____

Count the value of these notes.

㉖ [ ]

㉘ [ ]

㉗ [ ]

㉙ [ ]

㉚ How many $5 notes would you need to make $50? _____

㉛ How many $5 notes would you need to make $100? _____

㉜ How many $10 would you need to have $50? _____

㉝ How many $10 notes would you need to have $100? _____

Score 2 points for each correct answer! SCORE /66 (0-30) (32-60) (62-66)

Statistics

AC9M2ST02

Data representation

Farmer Ryan raised sheep and goats on his farm. He kept them together in four paddocks.

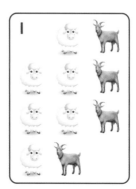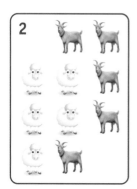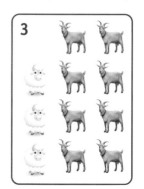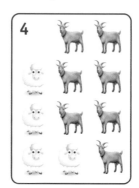

TARGETING HOMEWORK 2 © PASCAL PRESS ISBN 9781925726442

Use tally marks to count the number of sheep and the number of goats in each paddock. Cross out each sheep and goat as you count it. Write the totals in the boxes.

① **Paddock 1:** Sheep _____ [ ]   Goats _____ [ ]

② **Paddock 2:** Sheep _____ [ ]   Goats _____ [ ]

③ **Paddock 3:** Sheep _____ [ ]   Goats _____ [ ]

④ **Paddock 4:** Sheep _____ [ ]   Goats _____ [ ]

⑤ Present the information on this graph.

8								
7								
6								
5								
4								
3								
2								
1								
	Sheep	Goats	Sheep	Goats	Sheep	Goats	Sheep	Goats
	Paddock 1		Paddock 2		Paddock 3		Paddock 4	

⑥ In which paddock did Farmer Ryan have the most sheep? _____

⑦ In which paddock did Farmer Ryan have the most goats? _____

⑧ In which paddock is there the same number of sheep and goats? _____

⑨ How many sheep does Farmer Ryan have altogether? _____

⑩ How many goats does Farmer Ryan have altogether? _____

Score 2 points for each correct answer!   SCORE   **/20**   (0-8) (10-14) (16-20)

Problem Solving

AC9M2N06

How much money?

① Sam had five coins in his pocket. No two coins were the same.
He didn't have a $1 coin.
How much money did he have?   _____

② Zane had 7 coins in his pocket. There were 3 pairs of coins and 1 on its own.
Altogether the coins added up to $5.10.
What coins did Zane have?   _____

TERM 2 MATHS

Grammar & Punctuation

AC9E2LA10, AC9E2LY12

Pronouns

Nouns are the **names** of people, places, things, ideas and feelings.
Sometimes we use **pronouns** in place of nouns, so that we don't have to repeat the nouns.

Choose pronouns from the box to complete these sentences.

Pronouns
I   me
we   us
you
he   him
she   her
they   them
it

① The man was tired. _____ had to put the box down.

② The man put the box down. _____ was very heavy.

③ The girl sat at the table. _____ was doing her homework.

④ This is my book. My grandmother gave it to _____.

⑤ Did you see the emus at the zoo? _____ were running fast.

Using capital letters for titles

Capital letters are used for the most important words in titles, including the titles of books, stories, poems, movies and video games. We also put these titles in *italics*.
For example: *The Lost Dog*, *Goldilocks and the Three Bears*.

Circle the main words in each title and then write the title correctly.

⑥ the bear and the magic pot _____

⑦ whales and other mammals _____

⑧ australia's dinosaurs _____

Making nouns from verbs

We can add an **ending** to a **verb** to make a **noun** that means **'one who ...'**
We usually add **or** to words with two or more syllables.
For example, a **visitor** is one who **visits** and a **survivor** is one who **survives**.

Add or to the end of these verbs to make a noun. Explain the meaning.

	Verb	Noun (add or)	Meaning
⑨	act	_____	one who _____
⑩	invent	_____	one who _____
⑪	narrate	_____	one who _____
⑫	direct	_____	one who _____

Score 2 points for each correct answer!

SCORE | /24 (0-10) (12-18) (20-24)

Long vowel sounds – ow, oy, eer, air, our

Read the words in these lists. The words in each list have the same vowel sound.

long ow as in cow	long oy as in boy	long eer as in deer	long air as in hair	long our as in four
out	toy	dear	there	soar
how	void	fear	fair	pour
brown	coy	beard	lair	your
trout	annoy	seer	pair	fourth
found	voice	peer	their	court
bout	toil	hear	stare	course
pout	toilet	near	bare	mourn
mouth	royal	tear	where	flavour
down	foil	clear	air	favourite
frown	ploy	steer	care	neighbour

TERM 2 ENGLISH

Choose words from the lists to complete these sentences.

① The boy _____ his lost library book under the bed.

② The speaker's _____ could not be heard over the loud music.

③ The brave children said, "Have no _____. We will protect you."

④ The girl did not remember _____ she had put her hat.

⑤ My next door _____ has a friendly dog.

⑥ It is important to close your _____ when you are eating.

⑦ The toddler played happily with the new _____ all afternoon.

⑧ The boy was sad and a big _____ rolled down his cheek.

⑨ It is rude to _____ at other people.

⑩ My _____ colour is blue.

Circle the word that has a different vowel sound.

⑪ out   cow   heard   found

⑫ hear   there   where   stare

⑬ fourth   tour   you   your

⑭ toil   care   coil   boy

⑮ fair   care   clear   pair

Score 2 points for each correct answer!

SCORE **/30**   0-12   14-24   26-30

Trace the words. Start at the star. Follow the arrows.

This pair of

shoes is brown.

TERM 2 ENGLISH

Reading & Comprehension

Informative text – Description

AC9E2LA03, AC9E2LA05, AC9E2LA08, AC9E2LY03, AC9E2LY05

www.lostpets1.com.au

Lost Bird in Rosehill
Have you seen our bird?

Benny, our pet budgie, escaped last week when someone left the cage door open. (It wasn't me. It was my little brother.) We would really like to get him back. He likes to eat seeds out of our hands and he whistles all the time.

Suburb: Rosehill   **Missing since:** 30 November

Name: Benny   **Type:** bird

Breed: budgie   **Age:** 4 years

Microchip: yes   **Gender:** male

Colour: mauve with a blue tail

Click here to report

Write or tick the correct answer.

①   What is the notice about?

☐ a a lost bird

☐ b a bird for sale

☐ c a found bird

☐ d an injured bird

②   How was the bird lost?

☐ a It flew away when they were cleaning the cage.

☐ b It flew away when they were taking it for a walk.

☐ c It flew away when the cage door was open.

☐ d Somebody stole it.

TARGETING HOMEWORK 2 © PASCAL PRESS ISBN 9781925726442

③ What colour is the bird?

☐ **a** white   ☐ **c** green

☐ **b** yellow   ☐ **d** mauve

④ What is the bird's name?

☐ **a** Budgie   ☐ **c** Benny

☐ **b** Budgerigar   ☐ **d** Bird

⑤ What does the bird like to do?

☐ **a** fly

☐ **b** dance

☐ **c** eat seeds from our hands

☐ **d** eat chips

⑥ Where would you see this notice?

☐ **a** on a post in the street

☐ **b** in a pet shop window

☐ **c** at the vet

☐ **d** on the computer

⑦ What do you do if you find the pet?

☐ **a** Click on the link.

☐ **b** Phone the number.

☐ **c** Tell the police.

☐ **d** Take it to the pet shop.

⑧ Why would the bird have a microchip?

☐ **a** because it likes to eat small chips

☐ **b** to help find it if it's lost

☐ **c** to identify the owner when it is found

☐ **d** so it can listen to songs to whistle

⑨ Where might the bird be found?

☐ **a** only in Rosehill

☐ **b** in suburbs near Rosehill

☐ **c** far away from Rosehill

☐ **d** anywhere

⑩ What will the owners have to do to stop their bird from escaping again?

_____

_____

_____

TERM 2 ENGLISH

Score 2 points for each correct answer!   **SCORE**   **/20**   0-8   10-14   16-20

My Book Review

Title _____

Author _____

Colour stars to show your rating: ☆ ☆ ☆ ☆ ☆

Boring   Great!

Comment _____

_____

Number & Algebra

AC9M2N01, AC9M2N02, AC9M2N03, AC9M2N05, AC9M2N06, AC9M2A01

Numbers over 100

Write the missing numbers. Circle the number to tell how you are counting.
Circle F if you are counting forwards. Circle B if you are counting backwards.

① 27, 28, 29, _____, _____, _____, _____, 34, _____

   Counting (F) B   **in** (1s) 2s 3s 5s 10s

② 45, 50, 55, _____, _____, _____, _____, 80, _____

   Counting F B   **in** 1s 2s 3s 5s 10s

③ 90, 80, 70, _____, _____, _____, _____, 20, _____

   Counting F B   **in** 1s 2s 3s 5s 10s

④ 33, 36, 39, _____, _____, _____, _____, 54, _____

   Counting F B   **in** 1s 2s 3s 5s 10s

⑤ 88, 86, 84, _____, _____, _____, _____, 74 _____

   Counting F B   **in** 1s 2s 3s 5s 10s

Write these numbers in order from **smallest** to **largest**.

⑥ 276   854   576   342   139

   _____, _____, _____, _____, _____

⑦ 92   209   920   902   220

   _____, _____, _____, _____, _____

⑧ 634   364   420   237   546

   _____, _____, _____, _____, _____

⑨ 167   176   106   170   160

   _____, _____, _____, _____, _____

⑩ 956   965   999   901   919

   _____, _____, _____, _____, _____

Circle the **largest** number.

⑪ 453   534   435   345   354   ⑬ 629   269   692   926   962

⑫ 287   782   872   278   827   ⑭ 913   319   139   193   391

TARGETING HOMEWORK 2 © PASCAL PRESS ISBN 9781925726442

TERM 2 MATHS

Show these numbers on the abacuses.

⑮ 456

⑯ 725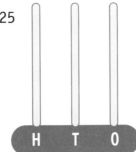

⑰ 364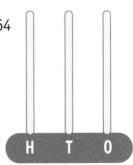

Write the numbers.

⑱ 3 hundreds + 4 tens + 2 ones = _____

⑳ 5 hundreds + 1 ten + 7 ones = _____

⑲ 8 hundreds + 2 tens + 6 ones = _____

㉑ 4 hundreds + 3 tens + 1 one = _____

Look at this array.
It has 3 rows with 4 stars in each row, or 4 columns with 3 stars in each column.

3 rows of 4 = 12

4 columns of 3 = 12

Draw boxes around these arrays to show the rows and columns. Write the two facts.

㉒

_____ rows of _____ = _____

_____ columns of _____ = _____

㉓

_____ rows of _____ = _____

_____ columns of _____ = _____

Fractions – quarters

 Hana and Jamie made a pizza to share.
They cut it in **half** so they could have half each.
Their friends Ali and Sarah came along. They wanted some pizza too.
"We can cut the pizza into four equal pieces so we all have
one quarter each," said Hana. So that is what they did.

Half is when we cut one whole into **two equal pieces**.

Quarters is when we cut one whole into **four equal pieces**.

Tick the shapes that are cut into quarters. Colour one quarter of each of those shapes.

 ㉔ 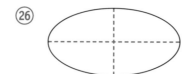 ㉖ 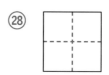 ㉘

㉕ ㉗ ㉙

TERM 2 MATHS

Hana, Jamie, Ali and Sarah baked **12 cookies**.
They shared the cookies so they had **one quarter** each.

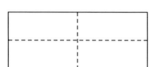 

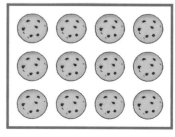

One quarter of 12 is 3.

Share these toys so that each child has one quarter each.
Draw the toys that each child has. Cross off the toys as you share them.

㉚

Hana	Jamie	Ali	Sarah

㉛

Hana	Jamie	Ali	Sarah

㉜

Hana	Jamie	Ali	Sarah

Score 2 points for each correct answer! SCORE **/64** (0-30) (32-58) (60-64)

Measurement & Space

Months of the year

One year has 365 days.
It is divided into 12 calendar months.
Each month has 30 or 31 days, except for February
which has 28 days and 29 days during a leap year.

January	February	March	April
May	June	July	August
September	October	November	December

Here is a rhyme to help you
remember the numbers of days.

Thirty days has September,
April, June and November.
All the rest have 31,
Except February alone
Which has 28
Or 29 each leap year.

① What is the first month of the calendar year? _____

② What is the last month of the calendar year? _____

③ What month comes after June? _____

④ What month comes before November? _____

⑤ What month comes between July and September? _____

⑥ What month comes after December? _____

⑦ What is the shortest month? _____

⑧ How many months have exactly 30 days? _____

⑨ How many months have 31 days? _____

Score 2 points
for each
correct answer!

SCORE

/18   0-6   8-14   16-18

Problem Solving

AC9M2M03

There are 6 mistakes on this calendar. Can you find them all?
Circle and correct them.

February 2020

Saturday	Monday	Thursday	Wednesday	Tuesday	Friday	Saturday
	1	2	3	4	5	6
7	8	9	10	11	12	10
14	15	26	17	18	19	20
21	22	23	24	25	26	27
28	29	30				

Grammar & Punctuation

Common nouns are the names of people, places and things.

Abstract nouns are the names of ideas and feelings.

Proper nouns are the names of specific people, places and things.
A proper noun begins with a **capital letter**.

Circle the nouns in these sentences.

① The big brown bear stole the honey from the beehive.

② The giant kangaroo bounced easily over the fence.

③ Max gave his homework to Mr Ricci this morning.

④ The fear of making a mistake stopped the girl from trying new things.

⑤ The excitement about the holidays could be heard all over the playground.

⑥ The helicopter hovered above the Sydney Harbour Bridge.

Adjectives describe or give more information to nouns.
Circle the adjectives in these sentences.

⑦ The tall vase is filled with beautiful flowers from the front garden.

⑧ The happy children watched the clever clown perform his magic tricks.

⑨ A deep river flowed past the tiny town in the hidden valley.

⑩ The frightened piglet squealed loudly when the big dogs barked.

Adverbs tell more about a verb. They often end with ly.
Circle the adverbs in these sentences.

⑪ The tiger moved silently through the jungle.

⑫ The people ran quickly from door to door with the news.

⑬ The children sat quietly while the teacher read to them.

⑭ The researchers worked patiently to find a cure for the disease.

Tick the nouns that mean 'one who'. Cross the other words.

⑮ ☐ water ⑱ ☐ actor ㉑ ☐ survivor ㉓ ☐ dancer

⑯ ☐ swimmer ⑲ ☐ bigger ㉒ ☐ conductor ㉔ ☐ speaker

⑰ ☐ feather ⑳ ☐ cleaner

Score 2 points for each correct answer! **SCORE** **/48** (0-22) (24-42) (44-48)

Circle the word that has a different vowel sound.

① cry fly die play

② grow snow brown toe

③ cow glow down how

④ do moon glue look

⑤ hoop shook put cook

⑥ mouse cloud blow cow

⑦ toy oil point paint

⑧ card calf war shark

⑨ where were germ fern

⑩ shirt surf herd cork

⑪ burp more door sport

⑫ dear fear stare seer

⑬ fair here pear there

⑭ four your door you

Write the correct word to complete these sentences.

⑮ I use my towel to _____ myself after a swim. (drie or dry)

⑯ My paper was wet because I used too much _____. (glue or blue)

⑰ The girl floated in the _____ on a blow-up mattress. (pull or pool)

⑱ The children were very _____ of their work. (prowd or proud)

⑲ The _____ was ready for the trip into space.
(astronaut or astronort)

⑳ We play soccer every _____. (Saturday or Saterday)

㉑ The _____ girl got a new bike from her parents.
(berthday or birthday)

㉒ The man said he didn't know _____ his keys were. (wear or where)

㉓ I need a new _____ of shoes for school this year. (pair or pear)

㉔ Mum told me to _____ myself a glass of juice. (pour or poor)

Tick the words that have the ow sound, as in cow. Cross the words that do not.

㉕ ☐ frown

㉖ ☐ you

㉗ ☐ your

㉘ ☐ mouth

㉙ ☐ fort

㉚ ☐ pout

㉛ ☐ found

㉜ ☐ corn

㉝ ☐ yawn

㉞ ☐ frown

㉟ ☐ four

㊱ ☐ glow

㊲ ☐ bout

㊳ ☐ how

㊴ ☐ mow

㊵ ☐ now

Score 2 points
for each
correct answer!

SCORE **/80** 0-38 40-74 76-80

Number & Algebra

Write the missing numbers.
Circle **F** if you are counting **forwards**. Circle **B** if you are counting **backwards**.
Then circle the number to tell how you are counting.

① 10, 20, 30, _____, _____, _____, _____, _____

I am counting F B   in 1s   2s   3s   5s   10s   100s

② 102, 104, 106, _____, _____, _____, _____, _____

I am counting F B   in 1s   2s   3s   5s   10s   100s

③ 137, 136, 135, _____, _____, _____, _____, _____

I am counting F B   in 1s   2s   3s   5s   10s   100s

④ 55, 60, 65, _____, _____, _____, _____, _____, _____

I am counting F B   in 1s   2s   3s   5s   10s   100s

⑤ 88, 86, 84, _____, _____, _____, _____, _____, _____

I am counting F B   in 1s   2s   3s   5s   10s   100s

⑥ 150, 250, 350, _____, _____, _____, _____, _____, _____

I am counting F B   in 1s   2s   3s   5s   10s   100s

Write how many hundreds, tens and ones. Then write the number.

⑦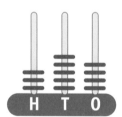

_____ hundreds, _____ tens, _____ ones

= _____

⑧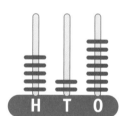

_____ hundreds, _____ tens, _____ ones

= _____

Show these numbers on the abacuses.

⑨ 617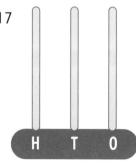

⑩ 283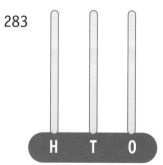

TARGETING HOMEWORK 2 © PASCAL PRESS ISBN 9781925726442

⑪

_____ rows of _____ = _____

_____ columns of _____ = _____

⑫

★ ★ ★ ★
★ ★ ★ ★

_____ rows of _____ = _____

_____ columns of _____ = _____

⑬ Tick the box with the most money.

a

b

c

TERM 2 MATHS

Score 2 points for each correct answer!

SCORE

/ 26   (0-10)   (12-20)   (22-26)

Measurement & Space

Write the names beside the correct shape:
triangle, rhombus, rectangle, circle, square, kite.

① ▢ _____

④ ◺ _____

② ◁ _____

⑤ ▱ _____

③ ▭ _____

⑥ ◯ _____

Draw the hands to show the time.

⑦ quarter past 5

⑧ quarter past 9

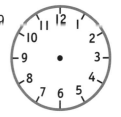

Score 2 points for each correct answer!

SCORE

/ 16   (0-6)   (8-12)   (14-16)

TERM 3 ENGLISH

Articles

> The three **articles** are **a, an** and **the**. They are words that come before a **noun**.
>
> Use **a** and **an** with **singular** (just one) nouns: a cat, an apple.
> **a** and **an** refer to **any** cat or **any** apple.
>
> Use **a** when the next word begins with a **consonant**: **a** cat or **a** crunchy apple.
> Use **an** when the next word begins with a **vowel**: **an** apple or **an** angry cat.
>
> Use **the** with both **singular** (just one) and **plural** (more than one) nouns: **the** cat, **the** cats.
> **the** refers to a **particular** cat or cats.

Circle the articles in these sentences.

①   I saw a girl running down the street.

②   The cook at the cafe baked a big chocolate cake.

③   Mai had a party at the skate park for her birthday.

④   Tema had an apple and an orange in his lunch.

Write the missing articles in these sentences.

⑤   Tema is _____ fast runner.

⑥   Sarah is _____ fastest runner in _____ class.

⑦   I saw _____ emu at _____ zoo on Saturday.

⑧   _____ blue whale is _____ largest animal that ever lived.

Alphabetical order

> a b c d e f g h i j k l m n o p q r s t u v w x y z
>
> When words are written in **alphabetical order**, they match the order of the letters
> in the **alphabet**. Like this: **a**pple, **b**ear, **d**oor, **e**gg, **t**easpoon, **w**alk.
>
> **Alphabetical order** is used in dictionaries, indexes and glossaries as well as class rolls.

Write these words in alphabetical order.

⑨   car, many, some, bat, helicopter

_____

⑩   spoon, fork, cake, money, zoo

_____

Score 2 points
for each
correct answer!

SCORE

/20   (0-8)   (10-14)   (16-20)

TARGETING HOMEWORK 2 © PASCAL PRESS ISBN 9781925726442

AC9E2LY09, AC9E2LY10

Consonant digraphs

Write the letters to make new words. Read the words.

① **sh** as in sh**ell**

sh op	ow

	sh	
ine		ape
ack		ark

ut	ip

② **wh** as in wh**ale**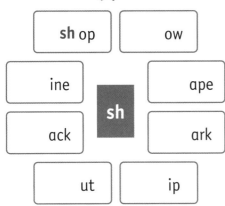

ine	ite

	wh	
eat		en
ip		at

eel	istle

③ **th** as in th**ree**

ing	ank

	th	
ick		ink
orn		islle

in	irsty

④ **ch** as in ch**ips**

op	at

	ch	
ick		ance
eese		ime

ain	amp

⑤ **qu** as in qu**een**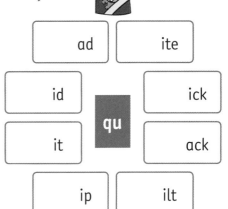

ad	ite

	qu	
id		ick
it		ack

ip	ilt

⑥ **ck** as in clo**ck**

bla	so

	ck	
plu		chi
ro		che

tru	thi

TERM 3 ENGLISH

Score 2 points
for each
correct answer!

SCORE **/12** (0-4) (6-8) (10-12)

Imaginative text – Narrative

A Trip to the Cake Shop

Mr Delgado wanted to surprise Mrs Delgado with her favourite berry and cream cake for morning tea.

The shop that made the best berry and cream cake was on the other side of town.

Mr Delgado got into his car to drive to the cake shop. The car would not start.

"Oh well," he said. "Looks like I'll have to catch the bus."

But there were no more buses.

"Oh well," said Mr Delgado. "Looks like I will have to catch the train."

But there were long train delays.

"Oh well," said Mr Delgado. "Looks like I'll have to walk to the cake shop."

It had been a long time since Mr Delgado had walked across town.

Mr Delgado got lost. It took him a long time to find his way to the cake shop. When he got there, he raced inside.

"One berry and cream cake, please," said Mr Delgado, huffing and puffing.

"Sorry, all sold out," said the cake maker. "We've been very busy today. I just sold the last one."

Source: Storylands Larkin Street, *A Trip to the Cake Shop*, Blake Education

Write or tick the correct answer.

① What did Mr Delgado want to buy for morning tea?

☐ **a** a berry and cream cake

☐ **b** strawberries and cream

☐ **c** a chocolate cake

☐ **d** doughnuts

② How did Mr Delgado get to the cake shop?

☐ **a** in his car ☐ **c** on a bus

☐ **b** by walking ☐ **d** on a train

③ Why did Mr Delgado want to buy the cake?

☐ **a** because it was his favourite

☐ **b** because it was his daughter's favourite

☐ **c** because it was his wife's favourite

☐ **d** because he was hungry

④ Where was the cake shop?

☐ **a** in another town

☐ **b** on the other side of town

☐ **c** near the train station

☐ **d** in the city centre

TERM 3 ENGLISH

⑤ Why didn't Mr Delgado drive to the shop?

☐ **a** His car wouldn't start.

☐ **b** Mrs Delgado was out in the car.

☐ **c** He wasn't allowed to drive.

☐ **d** He didn't like driving.

⑥ What happened to Mr Delgado on the way to the shop?

☐ **a** He saw a friend.

☐ **b** He got lost.

☐ **c** He lost his wallet.

☐ **d** He waited at the bus stop.

⑦ Why was Mr Delgado huffing and puffing when he got to the shop?

☐ **a** He was cross that he had to walk.

☐ **b** He was tired from walking a long way.

☐ **c** He didn't like the cake maker.

☐ **d** He wanted the cake maker to feel sorry for him.

⑧ Why couldn't Mr Delgado buy a berry and cream cake?

☐ **a** The cake maker didn't bake any that day.

☐ **b** The cake maker doesn't bake them anymore.

☐ **c** The cake maker didn't want to sell one to Mr Delgado.

☐ **d** There were no berry and cream cakes left.

⑨ How do you think Mr Delgado felt when he couldn't buy a berry and cream cake?

☐ **a** angry

☐ **b** disappointed

☐ **c** happy

☐ **d** proud

⑩ What do you think Mr Delgado will do now?

_____

_____

Score 2 points for each correct answer! **SCORE** | **/ 20** (0-8) (10-14) (16-20)

My Book Review

Title _____

Author _____

Colour stars to show your rating. ☆ ☆ ☆ ☆ ☆

Boring   Great!

Comment _____

_____

Number & Algebra

AC9M2N01, AC9M2N02, AC9M2N05, AC9M2N06, AC9M2A01

Numbers over 100

① Count in twos. Cross off each pair of stars as you count. Write how many altogether.

stars

② The farmer has 3 sheep in each pen. Count in threes. Write the numbers as you count.

_____ _____ _____ _____ _____ _____ _____ _____

③ Count the fingers in fives. Write how many altogether.

fingers

④ Each bag holds 10 marbles. Count the marbles in tens. Write how many altogether.

marbles

⑤ Each box contains 100 paperclips. Count the paperclips in 100s.
Write the numbers as you count.

_____ _____ _____ _____ _____ _____ _____ _____ _____ _____

paperclips

⑥ Write the number that is 1 more than 273. Then continue counting in 1s.

_____, _____, _____, _____

⑦ Write the number that is 2 more than 273. Then continue counting in 2s.

_____, _____, _____, _____

⑧ Write the number that is 5 more than 273. Then continue counting in 5s.

_____, _____, _____, _____

TARGETING HOMEWORK 2 © PASCAL PRESS ISBN 9781925726442

⑨ Write the number that is 10 more than 273. Then continue counting in 10s.

_____, _____, _____, _____

⑩ Write the number that is 100 more than 273. Then continue counting in 100s.

_____, _____, _____, _____

Write the largest and smallest numbers you can using these digits: 7 3 9
Show the numbers on the abacus. Write how many hundreds, tens and ones.

⑪ largest number:

_____

H T O

_____ hundreds, _____ tens, _____ ones

⑫ smallest number:

_____

H T O

_____ hundreds, _____ tens, _____ ones

⑬ Zane, Sasha and Tema had 12 marbles altogether.
They shared the marbles so each had the same number.
Draw the marbles in the bags.
Cross off the marbles as you share them.
Write how many marbles each child has.

Sasha

Tema

Zane

12 marbles shared between 3 children gives them _____ marbles each.

⑭ The baker made 12 cakes. He packaged them equally into 4 boxes.
Draw the cakes in the boxes. Cross off the cakes as you share them.
Write how many cakes in each box.

12 cakes packaged into 4 boxes makes _____ cakes in each box.

Score 2 points for each correct answer!   SCORE **/28**   0-12   14-22   24-28

Capacity

Sam's brother had been playing in the wading pool.
It was Sam's job to empty the pool.

He had to put the pool water into a watering
can and use it to water the garden.

Sam had a teaspoon, a plastic drinking cup
and a toy bucket. What should
he use to fill the watering can?

objects to use

watering can to fill

① Circle the object that Sam
should use to fill the
watering can the fastest.

② Cross the object that would take the longest time to fill the watering can.

Ali poured 4 glasses of juice from this jug of
orange juice. Then the jug was empty.

③ If Ali had to share the juice into 8 glasses,
how much would there be in each glass?
Colour the glasses to show your answer.

You use water in this activity, and it might
get messy. Ask an adult where you can do it.
You need a drinking cup, a large saucepan and
a large mixing bowl.

④ Estimate. Which do you think will hold more – the saucepan or the mixing bowl?

_____

⑤ Estimate. How many cups of water do you think it will take to fill the saucepan?

_____ cups

⑥ Estimate. How many cups of water do you think it will take to fill the mixing bowl?

_____ cups

⑦ Measure. Fill the cup with water, then pour the water into the saucepan.
Repeat until the saucepan is full. How many cups did you need?

_____ cups

TARGETING HOMEWORK 2 © PASCAL PRESS ISBN 9781925726442

⑧ Measure. Fill the cup with water, then pour the water into the mixing bowl. Repeat until the mixing bowl is full. How many cups did you need? _____ cups

⑨ Which holds more – the saucepan or the mixing bowl? _____

⑩ Were your estimates close? Answer yes or no. _____

3D shapes

Circle the correct name of each 3D shape.

⑪ 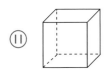 cube   cone   cylinder   sphere

⑫   cylinder   sphere   cone   cube

⑬ 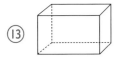 pyramid   triangular prism   cylinder   rectangular prism

⑭ 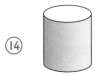 pyramid   rectangular prism   cylinder   sphere

⑮ 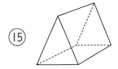 rectangular prism   triangular prism   pyramid   cube

⑯ 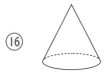 sphere   cylinder   cone   rectangular prism

⑰ 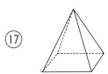 pyramid   cylinder   rectangular prism   triangular prism

Score 2 points for each correct answer!   SCORE   **/34**   0-14   16-28   30-34

Problem Solving

AC9M2N01

Number Riddles – What number am I?
Circle the correct answer in the box.

① | 45 55 47 48 49 50 46 44 |

② | 40 45 50 55 60 65 70 80 |

Clues: I am less than 50.
You can count me in 2s.
I am more than 46.

Clues: I am more than 50.
You can count me in 10s.
I am less than 70.

TERM 3 ENGLISH

Compound sentences – and

A **compound sentence** joins two **simple sentences** together.
Read these two simple sentences: Ari went to the shops. He bought a book.

We can use the word **and** to join the sentences together, like this:
Ari went to the shops **and** he bought a book.

Write the two simple sentences as a compound sentence, using the word and.

① John went to the beach. He had a swim.

_____

_____

② The little girl fell over. She hurt her knee.

_____

_____

Build these simple sentences into compound sentences, using the word and.

③ The children went home _____

④ The ball flew over the fence _____

⑤ The dog barked loudly _____

⑥ I did my homework _____

Alphabetical order

a b c d e f g h i j k l m n o p q r s t u v w x y z

When words are written in **alphabetical order**, they match the order of the letters
in the **alphabet**. When the first letter is the same, look at the second letter:
boat, **bu**s, **c**ar, **m**otorbike, **t**ruck, **v**an.

Alphabetical order is used in dictionaries, indexes and glossaries as well as class rolls.

Write these words in alphabetical order.

⑦ dragonfly, fly, bee, butterfly, ladybird

_____

⑧ Earth, Mercury, Mars, Jupiter, Saturn

_____

Score 2 points
for each
correct answer!
SCORE **/ 16** 0-6 8-12 14-16

TARGETING HOMEWORK 2 © PASCAL PRESS ISBN 9781925726442

Consonant blends

Write the letters to make new words. Read the words.

① scr as in scr**ew**

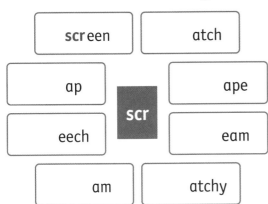

scr**een**	atch
ap	ape
eech	**scr**	eam
am	atchy

④ shr as in shr**ub**

ivel	ed
ew	ink
unk	**shr**	ank
imp	iek

② spl as in spl**ash**

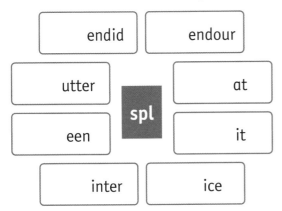

endid	endour
utter	at
een	**spl**	it
inter	ice

⑤ spr as in spr**int**

ee	ing
inkle	ain
ay	**spr**	ite
outs	ead

③ str as in str**ing**

etch	ap
aw	ain
ange	**str**	ip
ong	ipe

Choose a word from this page to complete each sentence.

⑥ A _____ is a small prawn.

⑦ The second pig made a house of

_____.

⑧ We came inside when it started to

_____.

⑨ Ducks like to _____ in muddy puddles.

⑩ I got a _____ on my knee when I fell over.

Score 2 points for each correct answer!

SCORE **/20** (0-8) (10-14) (16-20)

TERM 3 ENGLISH

Informative text – Report

Reptiles

There are four main groups of reptiles.

Snakes

Snakes do not have eyelids.

Some snakes have live babies and some lay eggs.

Snakes have a forked tongue.

Snakes have no legs.

Lizards

Some lizards have live babies and some lay eggs.

Almost all lizards have legs.

Lizards do not have a forked tongue.

Lizards have eyelids.

Crocodiles and alligators		
Saltwater Crocodile	Alligator	Freshwater Crocodile
V-shaped snout	U-shaped snout	Small, slender snout
Olive green/ brown	Blackish/grey	Light brown with dark bands
Bottom teeth show when jaw is closed	Bottom teeth don't show when jaw is closed	Slender, sharp teeth
Lives in salty or brackish water	Lives in freshwater lakes and swamps	Lives in freshwater and inland wetlands
Very aggressive	Less aggressive	Prefers small prey

Turtles and tortoises

Both **turtles** and **tortoises** lay eggs.

Both have shells on their backs.

Turtles live in water. They have flippers.

Tortoises live on the land. They have feet.

Source: Steve Parish First Facts, *Reptiles*, Pascal Press

Write or tick the correct answer.

① How many legs do snakes have? _____

② What is the same about turtles and tortoises?

◻ **a** They both live in the water.

◻ **c** They both have flippers.

◻ **b** They both lay eggs.

◻ **d** They can both swim.

3 What is the same about snakes and lizards?

☐ **a** They both have eyelids.

☐ **b** They don't have legs.

☐ **c** Some hatch out of eggs and some are born live.

☐ **d** They both have forked tongues.

4 What is the same about crocodiles and alligators?

☐ **a** They live in water.

☐ **b** They are very aggressive.

☐ **c** They live in fresh water.

☐ **d** They are olive green or brown.

5 Do all lizards have legs? _____

6 Write the sentence that tells you the answer to Question 5.

_____

_____

7 Which reptiles have shells and live on land?

_____

8 Which reptiles live in fresh water and inland wetlands?

☐ **a** tortoises

☐ **b** saltwater crocodiles

☐ **c** alligators

☐ **d** freshwater crocodiles

9 Which of these statements about turtles and tortoises is **not** true?

☐ **a** One lays eggs and the other one doesn't.

☐ **b** One has flippers and the other one doesn't.

☐ **c** One lives in water and the other one doesn't.

☐ **d** They both have shells.

10 Which animal is most dangerous?

☐ **a** tortoise

☐ **b** saltwater crocodile

☐ **c** alligator

☐ **d** freshwater alligator

Score 2 points for each correct answer!

SCORE **/20** (0-8) (10-14) (16-20)

TERM 3 ENGLISH

My Book Review

Title _____

Author _____

Colour stars to show your rating: ☆ ☆ ☆ ☆ ☆

Boring   Great!

Comment _____

_____

Numbers over 100

Write the missing numbers.
Circle F if you are counting forwards. Circle B if you are counting backwards.
Then circle the number to tell how you are counting.

TERM 3 MATHS

① 220, 222, 224, _____, _____, _____, _____, 234, _____

I am counting F B   in 1s   2s   3s   5s   10s   100s

② 465, 460, 455, _____, _____, _____, _____, 430, _____

I am counting F B   in 1s   2s   3s   5s   10s   100s

③ 15, 115, 215, _____, _____, _____, _____, 715, _____

I am counting F B   in 1s   2s   3s   5s   10s   100s

④ 93, 83, 73, _____, _____, _____, _____, 23, _____

I am counting F B   in 1s   2s   3s   5s   10s   100s

⑤ 232, 242, 252, _____, _____, _____, _____, 302, _____

I am counting F B   in 1s   2s   3s   5s   10s   100s

⑥ 333, 336, 339, _____, _____, _____, _____, 354, _____

I am counting F B   in 1s   2s   3s   5s   10s   100s

⑦ 37, 35, 33, 31, _____, _____, _____, _____, 21, _____

I am counting F B   in 1s   2s   3s   5s   10s   100s

⑧ 99, 100, 101, _____, _____, _____, _____, 106, _____

I am counting F B   in 1s   2s   3s   5s   10s   100s

⑨ 999, 899, 799, _____, _____, _____, _____, 299, _____

I am counting F B   in 1s   2s   3s   5s   10s   100s

⑩ 75, 80, 85, 90, _____, _____, _____, _____, 115, _____

I am counting F B   in 1s   2s   3s   5s   10s   100s

Circle the largest number. Underline the smallest number.

⑪ 279 972 297 927 792 729   ⑭ 634 364 643 436 463 346

⑫ 867 768 678 876 687 786   ⑮ 594 495 954 945 459 549

⑬ 123 312 213 321 132 231

TARGETING HOMEWORK 2 © PASCAL PRESS ISBN 9781925726442

Write the number.

(16)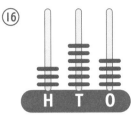

(18)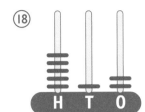

(20)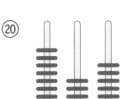

(17)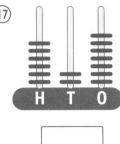

(19)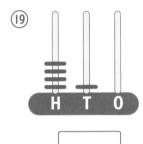

(21)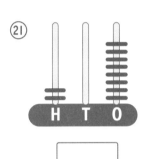

Expand these numbers.

(22) 372 = _____ hundreds, _____ tens, _____ ones

(23) 465 = _____ hundreds, _____ tens, _____ ones

(24) 193 = _____ hundred, _____ tens, _____ ones

(25) Share the apples onto the plates. Cross off the apples as you share them.

_____ apples shared onto _____ plates makes _____ apples on each plate.

(26) There were 6 flowers.
If each vase held three flowers,
how many vases were there?
Draw a picture to show your answer.

(27) Ten children played soccer.
There were two teams.
How many children were on each team?
Draw a picture to show your answer.

Score 2 points for each correct answer!

SCORE **/54** (0-24) (26-48) (50-54)

TERM 3 MATHS

Time - quarter to

The clock can be divided into 4 quarters.

When the big hand has gone one quarter of the way around the clock from 12, we say it is a **quarter past** the hour.

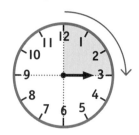

When it has gone halfway (2 quarters), we say it is **half past** the hour.

When it has gone 3 quarters of the way, it only has to go one more quarter until the next hour. We say it is a **quarter to** the hour.

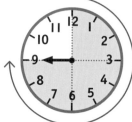

These clocks all show quarter to the hour. Complete the time.

①

quarter to ___

②

quarter to ___

③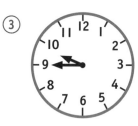

quarter to ___

④

quarter to ___

Draw the missing hand to show the time.

⑤ quarter to 6

⑥ quarter to 2

⑦ quarter to 3

⑧ quarter to 5

Draw the hands to show the time.

⑨ quarter to 11

⑩ quarter to 7

⑪ quarter to 12

⑫ quarter to 9

TARGETING HOMEWORK 2 © PASCAL PRESS ISBN 9781925726442

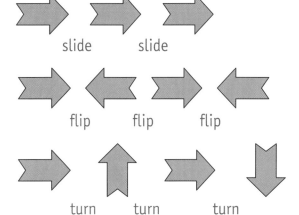

When an object **slides** to a new position, it does not change.

slide   slide

When an object **flips**, it becomes a mirror image.

flip   flip   flip

When an objects **turns**, it points in a different direction.

turn   turn   turn

Look at these pairs of pictures. Circle the word that tells how they have moved.

⑬   slide / flip / turn

⑭   slide / flip / turn

⑮   slide / flip / turn

⑯   slide / flip / turn

⑰   slide / flip / turn

⑱   slide / flip / turn

Score 2 points for each correct answer! SCORE **/36** (0-16) (18-30) (32-36)

Problem Solving

AC9M2N06

Solve this problem. You might like to draw a picture to help you work it out. Be careful – don't be tricked!

A farmer was walking to town to pick up his truck from the workshop.
On the way he met another farmer.
The farmer's horse was pulling a wagon full of cages.
In one cage there were 10 chickens.
In another cage there were 10 ducks,
and in another cage there were 10 geese.
The farmers stopped and spoke for a while,
then each went on their way.

Farmers, horses, chickens, ducks and geese – how many were going to town? _____

Compound sentences – but

> A **compound sentence** joins two **simple sentences** together.
> Read these two simple sentences: Ari went to the shops. He didn't buy anything.
>
> We can use the word **but** to join the sentences together, like this:
> Ari went to the shops **but** he didn't buy anything.
>
> **but** shows that the ideas are **different** from each other, or different from what you expect.

Write these two simple sentences as a compound sentence, using the word but.

① John went to the beach. He didn't have a swim.

_____

_____

② The little girl fell over. She didn't hurt herself.

_____

_____

Build these simple sentences into compound sentences, using the word but.

③ The children went home _____

④ The ball flew over the fence _____

⑤ I did my homework _____

Alphabetical order

> a b c d e f g h i j k l m n o p q r s t u v w x y z
>
> When words are written in **alphabetical order**, they match the order of the letters
> in the **alphabet**. When the first letter is the same, look at the second letter:
> m**a**st, m**e**ss, m**i**ss, m**o**st, m**u**st
>
> **Alphabetical order** is used in dictionaries, indexes and glossaries as well as class rolls.

Write these words in alphabetical order.

⑥ door, dragon, dance, dinner, deep

_____

⑦ lion, lemur, lamb, llama, lobster

_____

Score 2 points for each correct answer! SCORE **/14** (0-4) (6-10) (12-14)

90

TARGETING HOMEWORK 2 © PASCAL PRESS ISBN 9781925726442

TERM 3 ENGLISH

Trigraphs

ear Sometimes **ear** spells the sound like the **ear** you use to hear.	Sometimes **ear** spells the sound like in **wear**, the clothes you wear.

Look at the **ear words** in this table.
Colour the words that **rhyme with ear** blue.
Colour the words that **rhyme with wear** yellow.

① ear	④ tear	⑦ pear	⑩ hear	⑬ dear
② clear	⑤ gear	⑧ wear	⑪ near	⑭ year
③ spear	⑥ shear	⑨ rear	⑫ fear	⑮ bear

Sometimes a word can have either sound.
The way it is pronounced depends on the meaning. For example:

Be careful or you will **tear** the paper. (rhymes with **wear**)

The baby was starting to cry. She had a big **tear** on her cheek. (rhymes with **ear**)

tch At the end of a word, we often use the letters **tch** to spell the **ch sound**, as in **twitch**.

Write **tch** at the end of these words. Read the words.

⑯ ma_____   ⑳ scra_____   ㉓ ca_____

⑰ stre_____   ㉑ bo_____   ㉔ splo_____

⑱ wi_____   ㉒ fe_____   ㉕ clu_____

⑲ di_____

ure The letters **ure** spell the **or sound** as in **sure**. Are you **sure** you want to do that?

Write **ure** at the end of these words. Read the words.

㉖ c_____   ㉚ s_____   ㉝ treas_____

㉗ meas_____   ㉛ p_____   ㉞ mixt_____

㉘ pict_____   ㉜ pleas_____   ㉟ capt_____

㉙ mat_____

Score 2 points for each correct answer!

SCORE **/70** 0-32 34-64 66-70

TERM 3 ENGLISH

Trace the words. Start at the star. Follow the arrows.

I found the lost treasure last year.

Reading & Comprehension

AC9E2LA03, AC9E2LA08, AC9E2LE04, AC9E2LY05

Imaginative text – Poetry

My Shadow   by Robert Louis Stevenson

I have a little shadow that goes in and out with me,
And what can be the use of him is more than I can see.
He is very, very like me from the heels up to the head;
And I see him jump before me, when I jump into my bed.

The funniest thing about him is the way he likes to grow —
Not at all like proper children, which is always very slow;
For he sometimes shoots up taller like an india-rubber ball,
And he sometimes goes so little that there's none of him at all.

He hasn't got a notion of how children ought to play,
And can only make a fool of me in every sort of way.
He stays so close behind me, he's a coward you can see;
I'd think shame to stick to nursie as that shadow sticks to me!

One morning, very early, before the sun was up,
I rose and found the shining dew on every buttercup;
But my lazy little shadow, like an arrant sleepy-head,
Had stayed at home behind me and was fast asleep in bed.

Illustrator: Paul Lennon

Write or tick the correct answer.

① This poem is about

☐ **a** a lazy boy.

☐ **b** a shadow.

☐ **c** a ball.

☐ **d** some children.

② What does the poet think is funny about his shadow?

☐ **a** The way it jumps into bed.

☐ **b** The way it grows.

☐ **c** The way it bounces like a ball.

☐ **d** The way it stays in bed.

③ Why is the shadow described as a coward?

- ☐ **a** because it stays in bed
- ☐ **b** because it sometimes gets very small
- ☐ **c** because it always stays behind the boy
- ☐ **d** because it is very like the boy

④ Why do shadows sometimes get longer or shorter?

- ☐ **a** because the person gets taller or shorter
- ☐ **b** because of where the sun is in the sky
- ☐ **c** because the person stands up tall or squats down small
- ☐ **d** because they like playing ball

⑤ The poet said his shadow stayed in bed. Can shadows really stay in bed?

- ☐ **a** yes ☐ **b** no

⑥ Which word does the poet **not** use to describe his shadow?

- ☐ **a** lazy ☐ **c** funny
- ☐ **b** coward ☐ **d** proud

⑦ Why did the poet have no shadow when he got up early one morning?

- ☐ **a** There was dew on the buttercups.
- ☐ **b** His shadow liked to sleep in.
- ☐ **c** There was no sun to make a shadow.
- ☐ **d** The boy went out and didn't tell his shadow.

⑧ What does the poet say his shadow is like when it shoots up tall?

- ☐ **a** a coward ☐ **c** a ball
- ☐ **b** a buttercup ☐ **d** a bed

⑨ Find a word in the poem that rhymes with **me**. Then write three more words that rhyme with me.

_____

_____

⑩ Find a word in the poem that rhymes with **play**. Then write three more words that rhyme with play.

_____

_____

Score 2 points for each correct answer!

SCORE / 20 0-8 10-14 16-20

My Book Review

Title _____

Author _____

Colour stars to show your rating: ☆ ☆ ☆ ☆ ☆

Boring   Great!

Comment _____

_____

Number & Algebra

AC9M2N01, AC9M2N02, AC9M2N05, AC9M2N06, AC9M2A01

TERM 3 MATHS

Numbers over 100

1	2	③	4	5	6	7	8	9	10
11	12	13	14	15	16	17	18	19	20
21	22	23	24	25	26	27	28	29	30
31	32	33	34	35	36	37	38	39	40
41	42	43	44	45	46	47	48	49	50
51	52	53	54	55	56	57	58	59	60
61	62	63	64	65	66	67	68	69	70
71	72	73	74	75	76	77	78	79	80
81	82	83	84	85	86	87	88	89	90
91	92	93	94	95	96	97	98	99	100

① On the 100 grid, use green to colour the numbers you would count in 5s. The first one is coloured for you.

② Count back in 5s, starting from 100. Write the numbers.

100, _____, _____, _____, _____, _____, _____,

_____, _____, _____, _____, _____, _____, _____,

_____, _____, _____, _____, _____, _____

③ Count forwards in 5s, starting from 100. Write the numbers.

100, 105, _____, _____, _____, _____, _____, _____, _____, _____,

_____, _____, _____, _____, _____, _____, _____, _____, _____, _____

④ On the 100 grid, circle the numbers you would count in 3s. The first one is circled for you.

⑤ Tick the numbers that you count in both 3s and 5s. Write them here.

_____, _____, _____, _____, _____, _____

⑥ Write the next number you would count in both 3s and 5s. _____

Write these numbers in order from smallest to largest.

⑦ 753   357   735   537   375   573

_____, _____, _____, _____, _____, _____

⑧ 846   468   684   486   864   648

_____, _____, _____, _____, _____, _____

Arrange the 3 digits to make 6 different numbers. Write the numbers in order from smallest to largest.

⑨ **5 9 4**

_____, _____, _____, _____, _____, _____

⑩ **1 2 3**

_____, _____, _____, _____, _____, _____

TARGETING HOMEWORK 2 © PASCAL PRESS ISBN 9781925726442

Write the numbers shown with these blocks in three different ways.

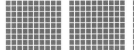

⑪ _____

⑫ _____ + _____

⑬ _____ tens, _____ ones

You partitioned the number into tens and ones.
We can also partition numbers in different ways, like this:

36	30 + 6
36	20 + 16
36	10 + 26

Partition these numbers in different ways.
The first one is done for you.

54	50 + 4

⑭ | 54 | |

⑮ | 54 | |

⑯ | 54 | |

⑰ | 54 | |

75	70 + 5

⑱ | 75 | |

⑲ | 75 | |

⑳ | 75 | |

㉑ | 75 | |

㉒ | 75 | |

Write the numbers shown with these blocks in three different ways.

㉓ _____

㉔ _____ + _____ + _____

㉕ _____ hundreds, _____ tens, _____ ones

You partitioned the number into tens and ones.
We can also partition numbers in different ways, like this:

347	300 + 40 + 7
347	200 + 140 + 7
347	100 + 240 + 7

Partition these numbers in different ways.
The first one is done for you.

615	600 + 10 + 5

㉖ | 615 | |

㉗ | 615 | |

㉘ | 615 | |

㉙ | 615 | |

㉚ | 615 | |

Look at these marbles.

(31) Circle groups of 2 marbles. How many groups did you make? _____

20 divided into groups of 2 makes _____ groups.

(32) Use a different colour to circle groups of 4. How many groups did you make? _____

20 divided into groups of 4 makes _____ groups.

(33) Use another colour to circle groups of 5. How many groups did you make? _____

20 divided into groups of 5 makes _____ groups.

(34) Use another colour to circle groups of 10. How many groups did you make? _____

20 divided into groups of 10 makes _____ groups.

Score 2 points for each correct answer!

SCORE **/68** (0-30) (32-62) (64-68)

Statistics

AC9M2ST01

Picture graphs

The children made a picture graph to show what they brought for fruit break.

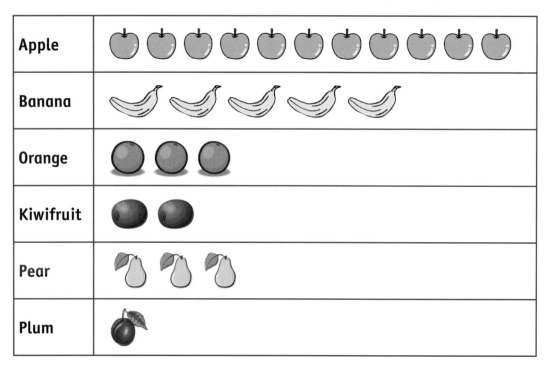

TARGETING HOMEWORK 2 © PASCAL PRESS ISBN 9781925726442

① Which was the most popular fruit? _____

② How many children had a banana? _____

③ How many children brought plums? _____

④ How many more children brought bananas than brought pears? _____

⑤ How many more children brought apples than brought bananas? _____

⑥ Were there fewer pears or kiwifruit? _____

⑦ Which two fruit were brought by the same number of children?

_____

⑧ Did more children have oranges or kiwifruit? _____

⑨ Which was the least popular fruit? _____

⑩ How many children are in the class? _____

Score 2 points for each correct answer! SCORE /20 0-8 10-14 16-20

Problem Solving

AC9M2N01

Follow the rules

Use the first two numbers in each row to make new numbers.
Follow these rules for each column.

A Write the larger number.

B Write the smaller number.

C Add the two numbers.

D Subtract the smaller number
from the larger number.

	A	B	C	D
6 and 4				
3 and 7				
8 and 2				
I and 9				

What do you notice about the numbers in each column?

Column A: _____

Column B: _____

Column C: _____

Column D: _____

What number is missing from the table? _____

Grammar & Punctuation

AC9E2LA06

Compound sentences – so

A **compound sentence** joins two **simple sentences** together.
Read these two simple sentences:
Ari couldn't find anything he wanted at the shops. He went home.

We can use the word **so** to join the sentences together, like this:
Ari couldn't find anything he wanted at the shops **so** he went home.

so shows that the ideas are **connected** because the first thing causes the second thing.

Write these two simple sentences as a compound sentence, using the word so.

① It was raining. John didn't go to the beach.

_____

_____

② Milo didn't come over. I watched TV by myself.

_____

_____

Build these simple sentences into compound sentences, using the word so.

③ I finished my homework _____

④ The baby fell over _____

Alphabetical order

a b c d e f g h i j k l m n o p q r s t u v w x y z

When words are written in **alphabetical order**, they match the order of the letters
in the **alphabet**. Some words begin with **silent letters**, like **knife** and **gnome**.
We still use these silent letters to put them in alphabetical order.

Alphabetical order is used in dictionaries, indexes and glossaries as well as class rolls.

Write these words in alphabetical order.

⑤ know, gnat, nice, lamb, kite, goat

_____

⑥ school, scamper, sign, singer, scrap

_____

Score 2 points for each correct answer! SCORE /12 0-4 6-8 10-12

98

TARGETING HOMEWORK 2 © PASCAL PRESS ISBN 9781925726442

Silent letters

Silent letters are used to spell words, but we don't hear these letters when we say the words aloud. A **silent letter** can be at the start of a word, in the middle or at the end.

Silent beginnings In the word **gnome**, the **g** is silent. We say it as if it were spelled **nome**.

 In the word **knight**, the **k** is silent. We say it as if it were spelled **night**.

Read the words. Circle the silent letter. Copy the words onto the lines below.

① knife

③ knee

⑤ know

_____

_____

_____

② gnat

④ wrap

⑥ hour

_____

_____

_____

Silent middle letters In the word **ghost**, the **h** is silent. We say it as if it were spelled **goast**.

 In the word **whistle**, the **t** is silent. We say it as if it were spelled **whissel**.

Read the words. Circle the silent letter. Copy the words onto the lines below.

⑦ could

⑨ two

⑪ sign

_____

_____

_____

⑧ school

⑩ calf

⑫ talk

_____

_____

_____

Silent endings In the word **thumb**, the **b** is silent. We say it as if it were spelled **thum**.

 In the word **comb**, the **b** is silent. We say it as if it was spelled **coam**.

Read the words. Circle the silent letter. Copy the words onto the lines below.

⑬ bomb

⑮ climb

⑰ lamb

_____

_____

_____

⑭ limb

⑯ tomb

⑱ crumb

_____

_____

_____

Score 2 points for each correct answer!

SCORE **/36**

TERM 3 ENGLISH

Trace the words. Start at the star. Follow the arrows.

The boy hurt his
knee when he fell.

TERM 3 ENGLISH

Reading & Comprehension

AC9E2LA03, AC9E2LA08, AC9E2LY05

Informative text – Graph and diagram

Mammals

Mammals are warm-blooded.

This image shows the temperature in and around a lion's body.

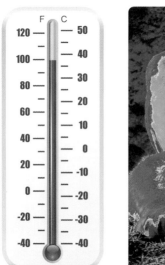

The body temperature of mammals is usually 36–39 °C (97–103 °F).

Mammals are warm-blooded because their body makes its own warmth.
Their body temperature stays about the same, whether the air around them
is hot or cold.

Source: Steve Parish First Facts, *Mammals*, Pascal Press

Write or tick the correct answer.

① The information in this graph and diagram is mainly about

☐ **a** warm-blooded animals.　　☐ **c** warm-blooded lions.

☐ **b** warm-blooded mammals.　　☐ **d** cold-blooded animals.

② The image of the lion shows

☐ **a** the temperature in and around the lion's body.

☐ **b** how an artist painted the lion.

☐ **c** how the lion looks in different coloured lights at night.

☐ **d** that the lion is ready to pounce.

③ What can warm-blooded animals do?

☐ **a** Hunt.

☐ **b** Read the temperature.

☐ **c** Make their own warmth.

☐ **d** Make the air warm or cold.

④ Is the lion's temperature the same all over its body?

☐ **a** yes   ☐ **b** no

⑤ What is the usual body temperature for mammals?

☐ **a** 36 °C

☐ **b** 38 °C

☐ **c** 37 °C

☐ **d** 36–39 °C

⑥ In Australia, we measure temperature in centigrade (C). In some other countries, temperature is measured in Fahrenheit (F). What is the usual temperature of mammals in Fahrenheit?

_____

⑦ What colour shows the warmest part of the lion's body?

☐ **a** pink   ☐ **c** yellow

☐ **b** green   ☐ **d** blue

⑧ What colour shows the coolest part of the lion's body?

☐ **a** pink   ☐ **c** yellow

☐ **b** green   ☐ **d** blue

⑨ Which part of the lion is warmest?

☐ **a** head   ☐ **c** body

☐ **b** legs   ☐ **d** mane

⑩ Which part of the lion is coolest?

☐ **a** head   ☐ **c** body

☐ **b** legs   ☐ **d** mane

TERM 3 ENGLISH

Score 2 points for each correct answer!   SCORE   **/20**   (0-8)   (10-14)   (16-20)

My Book Review

Title _____

Author _____

Colour stars to show your rating: ☆ ☆ ☆ ☆ ☆

Boring   Great!

Comment _____

_____

Numbers over 100

Start with 462.

1. Write the number that is 1 more. _____

2. Write the number that is 1 less. _____

3. Write the number that is 2 more. _____

4. Write the number that is 2 less. _____

5. Write the number that is 3 more. _____

6. Write the number that is 3 less. _____

7. Write the number that is 5 more. _____

8. Write the number that is 5 less. _____

9. Write the number that is 10 more. _____

10. Write the number that is 10 less. _____

11. Write the number that is 100 more. _____

12. Write the number that is 100 less. _____

13. Circle the numbers you would say when counting in 10s, starting at 54.

    45   450   540   124   64   74   334   94   104   400

Write the number shown on each abacus. Then write 1 more, 10 more and 100 more.

14.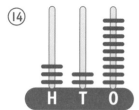

    _____

    1 more is _____

    10 more is _____

    100 more is _____

15.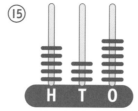

    _____

    1 more is _____

    10 more is _____

    100 more is _____

16.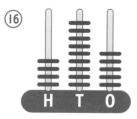

    _____

    1 more is _____

    10 more is _____

    100 more is _____

TARGETING HOMEWORK 2 © PASCAL PRESS ISBN 9781925726442

TERM 3 MATHS

Show these numbers on the abacuses.

⑰ 354

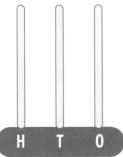

⑲ 278

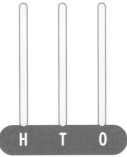

㉑ 721

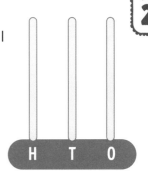

⑱ 10 more than 354

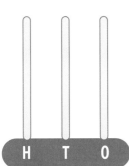

⑳ 100 more than 278

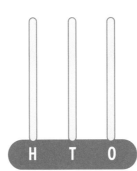

㉒ 1 more than 721

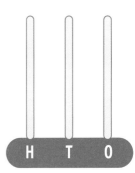

Look at these mangoes.

㉓ If you packed 2 mangoes into each bag, how many bags would you need? _____

20 divided into groups of 2 = _____   Are there any left over? _____

㉔ If you packed 4 mangoes into each bag, how many bags would you need? _____

20 divided into groups of 4 = _____   Are there any left over? _____

㉕ If you packed 3 mangoes into each bag, how many bags would you need? _____

20 divided into groups of 3 = _____   Are there any left over? _____

How many are left over? _____

Look at these horses.

㉖ If you put 3 horses in each paddock, how many paddocks would have horses? _____

15 divided into groups of 3 = _____   Are there any left over? _____

27. If you put 5 horses in each paddock, how many paddocks would have horses? _____

 15 divided into groups of 5 = _____   Are there any left over? _____

28. If you put 4 horses in each paddock, how many paddocks would have horses? _____

 15 divided into groups of 4 = _____   Are there any left over? _____

 How many are left over? _____

Fractions – eighths

half: one whole cut into 2 equal pieces.
quarter: one whole cut into 4 equal pieces.
eighth: one whole cut into 8 equal pieces.

Tick the shapes that are cut into eighths. Colour one eighth of each of those shapes.

29.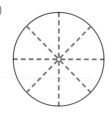

31.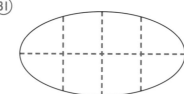

33.

30.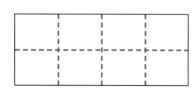

32.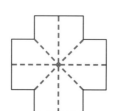

34.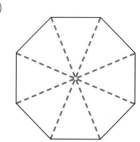

There were 8 children at a party.

35. Draw lines on this pizza so that each child gets one eighth.

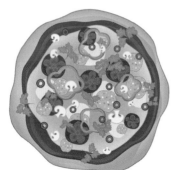

36. Now draw lines on this chocolate so that each child gets one eighth.

Score 2 points for each correct answer!   **SCORE** /72   0-34 36-66 68-72

TARGETING HOMEWORK 2 © PASCAL PRESS ISBN 9781925726442

The seasons

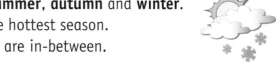

There are four **seasons** in each year – **spring**, **summer**, **autumn** and **winter**. Each season is three months long. Summer is the hottest season. Winter is the coldest season. Autumn and spring are in-between.

Australia is in the Southern Hemisphere where the seasons are:

Summer: December, January, February

Autumn: March, April, May

Winter: June, July, August

Spring: September, October, November

In the Northern Hemisphere, the seasons are in the opposite months:

Winter: December, January, February

Spring: March, April, May

Summer: June, July, August

Autumn: September, October, November

① When does summer begin in the Southern Hemisphere? _____

② What is the last month of winter in the Southern Hemisphere? _____

③ How long is summer? ___ months

④ When is it autumn in the Southern Hemisphere?

_____

⑤ When it is summer in the Southern Hemisphere, what is the season in the Northern Hemisphere? _____

⑥ When does summer begin in the Northern Hemisphere? _____

⑦ What is the last month of winter in the Northern Hemisphere? _____

⑧ In which season does it begin to cool down? _____

⑨ In which season does it begin to warm up?

_____

Score 2 points for each correct answer!

SCORE **/18** (0-6) (8-14) (16-18)

Problem Solving

AC9M2M02

These things have been cut in half.
Draw the other half to show what it looked like before it was cut.

①

②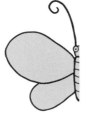

③

Grammar & Punctuation

Write the missing articles – a, an, the – in these sentences.

① I saw _____ bird in _____ tree over there.

② Sam had _____ apple and _____ banana for lunch.

③ We went to _____ beach and had _____ swim on the weekend.

④ Miss Hili told _____ boy to put _____ book on _____ shelf.

⑤ Tema saw _____ octopus and _____ starfish at _____ aquarium.

Write the two simple sentences as a compound sentence. Use and, but or so.

⑥ The shop was closed. Ari went home.

_____

_____

⑦ The baby was hungry. She started to cry.

_____

_____

⑧ Max looked everywhere. He couldn't find his book.

_____

_____

⑨ He turned off the light. He went to sleep.

_____

_____

Write these words in alphabetical order.

a b c d e f g h i j k l m n o p q r s t u v w x y z

⑩ goat, gone, ghost, game, gust

_____

⑪ knight, nine, know, nice, night

_____

Score 2 points for each correct answer! **SCORE** **/22** 0-8 10-16 18-22

TARGETING HOMEWORK 2 © PASCAL PRESS ISBN 9781925726442

Phonic Knowledge & Spelling

Read these words. The **consonant digraph** is **black**.

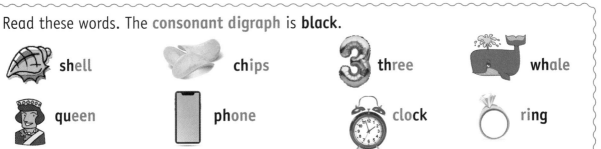

sh**ell**   **ch**ips   **th**ree   wh**ale**

qu**een**   **ph**one   clo**ck**   ri**ng**

Choose a **consonant digraph** from the box above to complete each word.

① _____ilt   ③ _____rone   ⑤ ele_____ant

② bla_____   ④ _____ark   ⑥ bli_____

Read these words. The **consonant blend** is **black**.

 screw   **shr**ub   **spl**ash   **spr**int   **str**ing

Choose a **consonant blend** from the box above to complete each word.

⑦ _____ip   ⑨ _____it   ⑪ _____iek

⑧ _____atch   ⑩ _____inkle   ⑫ _____ink

The **trigraph ear** has two sounds, as in **hear** and in **bear** .

Read this paragraph. Underline all the words with the trigraph **ear**.
Circle the words you have underlined that rhyme with **bear**.

⑬-㉕ Last year I camped in a forest near the beach. One day I went for a walk. I didn't
wear a raincoat because the sky was clear. I took all my gear in a backpack. When
I had gone a short way, I could hear something strange. A bear cub was crying.
There were tears on its face. I thought it might be hungry. I took a pear out of my
backpack and gave it to the cub. Then I ran back to camp in fear that its mother
might not be so sweet.

Circle the **silent letter** in each of these words.
It might be at the beginning, in the middle or at the end.

㉖ knife   ㉘ bomb   ㉚ sign

㉗ two   ㉙ gnat

Score 2 points
for each
correct answer!

SCORE /60   0-28   30-54   56-60

Number & Algebra

Write the missing numbers in these sequences. How are you counting?

① 227, 229, 231, _____, _____, _____, 239, _____, _____   Counting in _____

② 305, 315, 325, _____, _____, _____, 365, _____, _____   Counting in _____

③ 58, 158, 258, _____, _____, _____, 658, _____, _____   Counting in _____

④ 425, 430, 435, _____, _____, _____, 455, _____, _____   Counting in _____

⑤ 33, 36, 39, _____, _____, _____, 51, _____, _____   Counting in _____

Arrange the 3 digits to make 6 different numbers.
Write the numbers in order from smallest to largest.

⑥ **6 3 9**   _____, _____, _____, _____, _____, _____

⑦ **5 8 7**   _____, _____, _____, _____, _____, _____

Write the numbers shown with these blocks in three different ways.

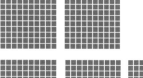

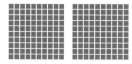 

⑪ _____

⑫ _____ + _____ + ____

⑬ ____ hundreds, ____ tens, ____ ones

⑧ _____

⑨ _____ + _____ + ____

⑩ ____ hundreds, ____ tens, ____ ones

Partition these numbers in different ways. The first one is done for you.

375	300 + 70 + 5
⑭ 375	
⑮ 375	

629	600 + 20 + 9
⑯ 629	
⑰ 629	
⑱ 629	
⑲ 629	
⑳ 629	

TARGETING HOMEWORK 2 © PASCAL PRESS ISBN 9781925726442

TERM 3 MATHS

㉑ Share these treats equally between Zane, Sasha, Tema and Sam.

_____ treats shared between _____ children gives them _____ each.

㉒ Look at these coins.
Three $1 coins were put into each piggy bank.

How many piggy banks are there? _____

18 divided into groups of 3 = _____

Are there any left over? _____

Score 2 points for each correct answer! **SCORE** /44 (0-20) (22-38) (40-44)

Measurement & Space

Time – hour, half past, quarter past, quarter to

Draw lines to match the times to the clocks.

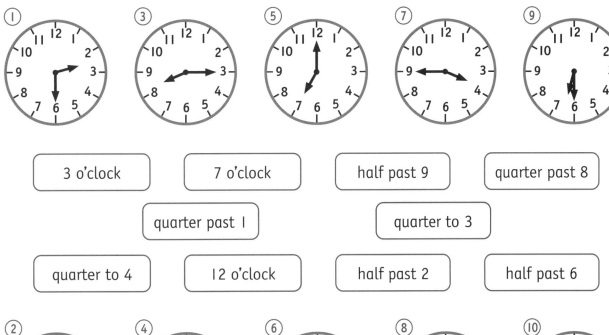

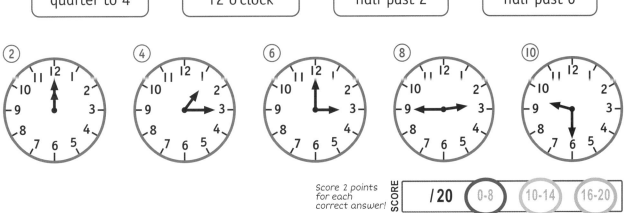

Score 2 points for each correct answer! **SCORE** /20 (0-8) (10-14) (16-20)

Grammar & Punctuation

AC9E2LA09

Synonyms

Words that are **synonyms** have nearly the same meaning. For example:
large and **big**   **tiny** and **small**   **beautiful** and **pretty**   **break** and **smash**

Circle the synonym for the first word.

① **sick**   well ill happy sad

② **giggle**   cry talk wink laugh

③ **happy**   joyful sad unhappy excited

④ **long**   tall lengthy short big

⑤ **shout**   whisper speak yell cry

Write a synonym for the underlined word. Choose words from the box.

cook   garbage   jump   present   road   rock   sleep   small   smart   young

⑥ _____ The boy took a tiny bite out of the apple.

⑦ _____ The baby lion was very cute.

⑧ _____ The clever girl answered all the questions correctly.

⑨ _____ The old man was very happy with his birthday gift.

⑩ _____ I will help Dad bake a cake this afternoon.

⑪ _____ I get annoyed when I see rubbish left on the beach.

⑫ _____ A frog can hop from rock to rock.

⑬ _____ The car sped along the highway.

⑭ _____ I was very tired, so I had a nap in the afternoon.

⑮ _____ The woman picked up a stone that was lying on the path.

Write your own synonym for these words.

⑯ speak   _____

⑰ fast   _____

⑱ freezing   _____

⑲ friend   _____

⑳ correct   _____

Score 2 points for each correct answer!

SCORE **/40** (0-18) (20-34) (36-40)

TARGETING HOMEWORK 2 © PASCAL PRESS ISBN 9781925726442

Syllables

Words are made up of **syllables**. **Every syllable** has a **vowel sound**.
You can **clap the syllables** in words.

Some words have **one syllable**: cat plane book shoe

Some words have **two syllables**: **rab**bit **do**nut **win**dow **pea**nut

These words have **three syllables**: **but**ter**fly** **al**pha**bet** **spa**ghet**ti**

This word has **four syllables**: **ca**ter**pil**lar

Some syllables break **between consonants**:

button = but + ton   kitten = kit + ten   bedroom = bed + room

It is easier to spell long words when you break them into syllables.

TERM 4 ENGLISH

Look at these words. Show how to break them into syllables.

① hiccup = _____ + _____

② magnet = _____ + _____

③ picnic = _____ + _____

④ ribbon = _____ + _____

⑤ happen = _____ + _____

⑥ butter = _____ + _____

Look at the pictures. Write the words. Break them into syllables to help.

⑦ _____

⑧ _____

⑨ _____

⑩ _____

⑪ _____

⑫ 100 _____

⑬ _____

⑭ _____

Read this paragraph. Circle the words that have two syllables.

⑮-㉕ The lazy carpenter opened his toolbox. He took out his hammer, his chisel and his screwdriver. He picked up a piece of timber. He hit a nail into the wood using his hammer. Then he hit his finger. "Ouch!" he said, and put his tools away.

Score 2 points for each correct answer!

SCORE / 50   (0-22)   (24-44)   (46-50)

Narrative text – Short story

TERM 4 ENGLISH

Buzz Boy's Favourites

Buzz Boy's room was messy with toys.

"I think it's time to throw out some of your old toys," said Buzz Boy's mother.

She handed him a box that had 'OUT' written in big letters on the side.

"Put all the toys you don't play with in the box," she said.

"But Mum," said Buzz Boy, "I can't throw out any toys. I like them all."

"No 'buts'," said his mother. "They can't all be your favourites."

Buzz Boy looked around his room. There were toys everywhere. They filled the cupboards and the bookshelves. They jammed the space under his bed. They piled out of boxes and onto the floor. But he didn't have any toys he wanted to put in the OUT box.

As Buzz Boy sorted the toys, he had an idea.

Source: Storylands Larkin Street, *Buzz Boy's Favourites*, Blake Education

Write or tick the correct answer.

① What did Buzz Boy's mother want him to do?

☐ **a** Tidy his room.

☐ **c** Play with his toys.

☐ **b** Throw out some toys.

☐ **d** Give his toys to his friends.

② What toys did Buzz Boy's mother want him to put in the OUT box?

☐ **a** all of them

☐ **c** the broken ones

☐ **b** the ones he doesn't play with anymore

☐ **d** his favourites

③ Which toys did Buzz Boy want to put in the box?

☐ **a** all of them

☐ **c** none of them

☐ **b** the ones he doesn't play with anymore

☐ **d** the broken ones

④ Why didn't Buzz Boy want to throw out any toys?

☐ a He was selfish and didn't want to share.

☐ b He liked them all.

☐ c He wanted to give the toys to his friends.

☐ d He wanted to play with them.

⑤ Where were Buzz Boy's toys?

☐ a stacked neatly on shelves

☐ b organised into boxes

☐ c arranged tidily in cupboards

☐ d everywhere

⑥ When his mother left the room, Buzz Boy started to

☐ a sort his toys.

☐ b play with his toys.

☐ c cry.

☐ d tidy his room.

⑦ How do you think Buzz Boy felt about throwing out some of his toys?

☐ a excited   ☐ c frightened

☐ b proud   ☐ d disappointed

⑧ Buzz Boy's mother told him to throw out his toys because

☐ a she was mean.

☐ b she didn't want Buzz Boy to have any toys.

☐ c she thought he had too many toys.

☐ d she was angry because he made so much mess.

⑨ Do you think Buzz Boy will put any of his toys in the OUT box?

☐ a yes   ☐ b no

⑩ Buzz Boy had an idea. What do you think his idea is?

_____

_____

TERM 4 ENGLISH

Score 2 points for each correct answer!

SCORE **/20**   0-8   10-14   16-20

My Book Review

Title _____

Author _____

Colour stars to show your rating: ☆ ☆ ☆ ☆ ☆

Boring   Great!

Comment _____

_____

Number & Algebra

AC9M2N01, AC9M2N02, AC9M2N03, AC9M2N04, AC9M2A02, AC9M2A03

Numbers over 100

① Write these numbers in order from **smallest to largest** (ascending order).

548   627   854   392   99   102   111   923   990   909

_____, _____, _____, _____, _____, _____, _____, _____, _____, _____

② Write these numbers in order from **largest to smallest** (descending order).

623   69   609   690   428   862   99   100   694   906

_____, _____, _____, _____, _____, _____, _____, _____, _____, _____

TERM 4 MATHS

Complete this table.

	100 less	10 less	1 less		1 more	10 more	100 more
③				509			
④				427			
⑤				650			
⑥				345			
⑦				194			

Complete this table.

	Blocks	Number	Expanded	H T O
⑧			____ + ____ + ____	____ hundreds ____ tens ____ ones
⑨		258	____ + ____ + ____	____ hundreds ____ tens ____ ones
⑩			300 + 70 + 5	____ hundreds ____ tens ____ ones
⑪			____ + ____ + ____	1 hundred 9 tens 2 ones

TARGETING HOMEWORK 2 © PASCAL PRESS ISBN 9781925726442

Doubles facts

Complete this table.

		Double	Half
⑫		Double 1 = ___	Half of 2 = ___
⑬		Double ___ = ___	Half of ___ = ___
⑭		Double ___ = ___	Half of ___ = ___
⑮		Double ___ = ___	Half of ___ = ___
⑯		Double ___ = _____	Half of _____ = ___
⑰		Double ___ = _____	Half of _____ = ___
⑱		Double ___ = _____	Half of _____ = ___
⑲		Double ___ = _____	Half of _____ = ___
⑳		Double ___ = _____	Half of _____ = ___
㉑		Double ___ = _____	Half of _____ = ___

TERM 4 MATHS

Write the addition or subtraction fact for each story. Then write the answer.

㉒ A woman was making animals from balloons at the fair.
She made ten animals in the morning and seven more in the afternoon.
How many balloons did she make?

_____

㉓ Nine children were playing hide and seek. Three children had been found.
How many still needed to be found?

_____

㉔ The football team scored 8 goals in the first half and 3 goals in the second half.
How many goals did they score all together?

_____

Score 2 points for each correct answer! **SCORE** **/48** 0-22 24-42 44-48

Mass

Look at these balance scales. Circle the heavier object. Tick the lighter object.

Look at these balance scales. The objects balance.

The children used blocks to balance each object.

 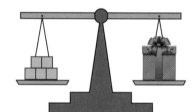

Draw the blocks the children would use to balance these objects.

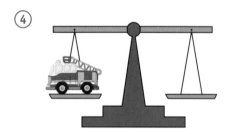 

⑥ Which object is heavier? Circle it.

⑦ How many blocks do you need
to balance this scale?
Draw the blocks.

TERM 4 MATHS

3D shapes

Complete the table to tell the number of faces, edges and corners.

	Shape	Faces	Edges	Corners
8				
9				
10				
11				

	Shape	Faces	Edges	Corners
12				
13				
14				

Score 2 points for each correct answer!

SCORE /28   0-12   14-22   24-28

Problem Solving

AC9M2N01, AC9M2SP02

100 square puzzles

Use the 100 square to complete the activities.

1. Colour the numbers in which the two digits add to 10.

2. What do you notice about the numbers?

_____

_____

3. Circle 86. Go up 3. Go right 3. Go down 3. Go left 3.

4. Where do you land? _____

5. What shape did you make?

_____

6. Circle 54. Go up 2. Go left 3. Go up 1. Go right 4.

7. Where do you land? _____

1	2	3	4	5	6	7	8	9	10
11	12	13	14	15	16	17	18	19	20
21	22	23	24	25	26	27	28	29	30
31	32	33	34	35	36	37	38	39	40
41	42	43	44	45	46	47	48	49	50
51	52	53	54	55	56	57	58	59	60
61	62	63	64	65	66	67	68	69	70
71	72	73	74	75	76	77	78	79	80
81	82	83	84	85	86	87	88	89	90
91	92	93	94	95	96	97	98	99	100

AC9E2LA09

Antonyms

Words that are **antonyms** have nearly the opposite meaning. For example:
large and **small**   **tiny** and **huge**   **beautiful** and **ugly**   **make** and **smash**

Circle the antonym for the first word.

① **healthy**   well ill happy sad

② **tall**   long high short big

③ **laugh**   cry talk wink chuckle

④ **happy**   joyful sad proud excited

⑤ **shout**   whisper speak yell cry

TERM 4 ENGLISH

Write an antonym for the underlined word. Choose words from the box.

| dirty | dry | easy | fast | happy | left | quiet | right | save | young |

⑥ _____ The old man went into the shop.

⑦ _____ The towel on the rail was wet.

⑧ _____ The sign on the road said to turn right.

⑨ _____ I will spend all the money I got for my birthday.

⑩ _____ The boy thought the work was very difficult.

⑪ _____ It makes me sad when we have to go to the park.

⑫ _____ The picnic table at the park was clean.

⑬ _____ The children were very noisy when the teacher left the room.

⑭ _____ The tortoise was very slow in the race.

⑮ _____ I got every question on the test wrong.

Write your own antonym for these words.

⑯ friend _____

⑰ poor _____

⑱ good _____

⑲ day _____

⑳ asleep _____

Score 2 points
for each
correct answer!

SCORE **/40**

TARGETING HOMEWORK 2 © PASCAL PRESS ISBN 9781925726442

Syllables

Some words break into **syllables** between **two consonants**, like **button** (but/ton) and **hammer** (ham/mer).

Some words do not have two consonants to break between.
They break **after the vowel** and **before the consonant**.

 donut = do/nut   peanut = pea/nut

Read these words. Write them using / to show the syllables.

① father = _____

② water = _____

③ moment = _____

④ token = _____

⑤ about = _____

⑥ donate = _____

TERM 4 ENGLISH

Look at the pictures. Write the words. Break them into syllables to help.

⑦ _____

⑧  _____

⑨  _____

⑩ _____

⑪  _____

⑫  _____

**Read the words in the box.
Count the syllables.
Write the words in the
correct part of the table.**

act	book	branch	butterfly	car	carpenter
chuckle	dancer	dragonfly	funny	head
pizza	platypus	sometimes	television

One syllable	Two syllables	More than two syllables
⑬	⑱	㉓
⑭	⑲	㉔
⑮	⑳	㉕
⑯	㉑	㉖
⑰	㉒	㉗

Score 2 points
for each
correct answer!

SCORE **/54** 0-24 26-48 50-54

UNIT 27

Trace the words. Start at the star. Follow the arrows.

The tiger saw the spider and jumped over the puddle.

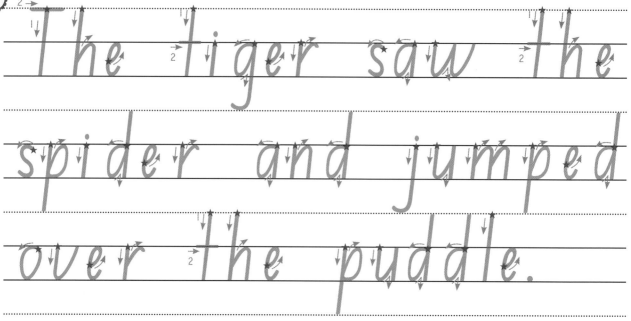

TERM 4 ENGLISH

Reading & Comprehension

Informative text – Glossary

AC9E2LA03, AC9E2LA05, AC9E2LY03, AC9E2LY05

Glossary

antennae (p 8, 11, 22) body parts that help insects smell and feel things around them

cold-blooded (p 5, 22) having a body that cannot make its own warmth

compound eyes (p 9, 22) eyes made up of several tiny parts that gather light

invertebrates (p 6, 19, 22) animals without a backbone

metamorphosis (p 13–16, 18) a series of changes in some animals as they grow into their adult form

pupa stage (p 18) a stage in the life of some insects when they are covered in a special case

skeleton (p 6) the structure that supports an animal's body

species (p 19) groups of animals that have certain common features

Source: Steve Parish First Facts, *Insects*, Pascal Press

Write or tick the correct answer.

① How are the words in the glossary arranged?

☐ **a** in alphabetical order

☐ **c** There is no order.

☐ **b** in the order of pages

☐ **d** from shortest to longest

② The purpose of a glossary is to

☐ **a** give you words to learn to spell.

☐ **b** explain the meaning of words.

☐ **c** tell you where to find more information in the book.

☐ **d** b. and c.

③ Which word in the glossary refers to animals with backbones?

☐ **a** cold-blooded

☐ **b** skeleton

☐ **c** metamorphosis

☐ **d** antennae

④ What happens to insects in the **pupa stage**?

☐ **a** Their pupils get bigger.

☐ **b** They perform on stage.

☐ **c** They are covered in a special case.

☐ **d** They die.

⑤ On what pages could you find out more about **metamorphosis**?

_____

⑥ If these words were added to the glossary, which would be listed first?

☐ **a** wings   ☐ **c** proboscis

☐ **b** chrysalis   ☐ **d** cocoon

⑦ What do insects use their **antennae** for?

_____

_____

⑧ According to the glossary, what is a **skeleton**?

_____

_____

⑨ What would you read about on page 8?

_____

⑩ What would you read about on page 9?

_____

TERM 4 ENGLISH

Score 2 points for each correct answer!   SCORE **/ 20**   0-8   10-14   16-20

My Book Review

Title _____

Author _____

Colour stars to show your rating: ☆ ☆ ☆ ☆ ☆

Boring   Great!

Comment _____

_____

AC9M2N01, AC9M2N02, AC9M2N05, AC9M2A01, AC9M2A03

Numbers over 100

Join the dots.

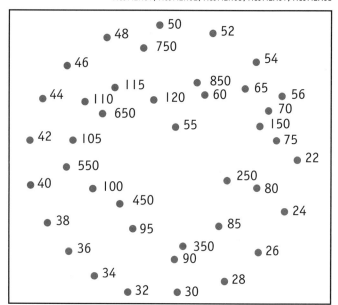

① Start at 22. Count in 2s and use green to join the dots.

When you reach 56, join it to 22.

What shape did you make?

_____

② Start at 55. Count in 5s and use red to join the dots.

When you reach 120, join it to 55.

What shape did you make?

_____

③ Start at 150. Count in 100s and use blue to join the dots.
When you reach 850, join it to 150. What shape did you make? _____

TERM 4 MATHS

Write the number that comes next.

④ 258, 259, 260, _____

⑤ 765, 770, 775, _____

⑥ 844, 843, 842, _____

⑦ 960, 950, 940, _____

⑧ 198, 199, 200, _____

⑨ 885, 890, 895, _____

Partition these numbers in different ways. The first one is done for you.

⑩

654	600 + 50 + 4
654	
654	
654	
654	

⑪

793	700 + 90 + 3
793	
793	
793	
793	

Write the numbers shown on these abacuses.

⑫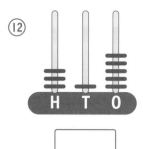

⑬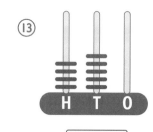

⑭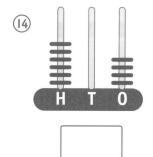

TARGETING HOMEWORK 2 © PASCAL PRESS ISBN 9781925726442

Multiplication

Look at this **array**.

We could say there are **3 rows of 4 stars**, or there are **4 columns of 3 stars**.

Either way, there are 12 stars altogether.

3 rows of 4 are 12.   4 columns of 3 are 12.
$3 \times 4 = 12$ $4 \times 3 = 12$

Write 2 multiplication facts for each array.

⑮
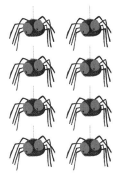

_____ × _____ = _____

_____ × _____ = _____

⑰

_____ × _____ = _____

_____ × _____ = _____

⑯

_____ × _____ = _____

_____ × _____ = _____

⑱

_____ × _____ = _____

_____ × _____ = _____

Circle the correct fact for each array.

⑲

2 × 5   3 × 5   3 + 5   5 × 4

⑳

5 + 4   6 × 5   3 × 5   4 × 5

Score 2 points for each correct answer!   SCORE   **/40**   0-18   20-34   36-40

Slides, flips and turns

**Look at the object on the left. Follow the instructions.
Draw the new object in the grid on the right.**

① slide

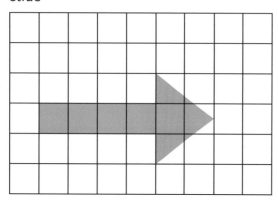 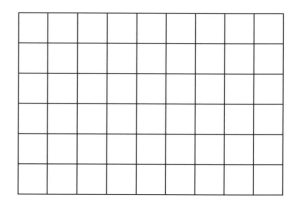

② turn

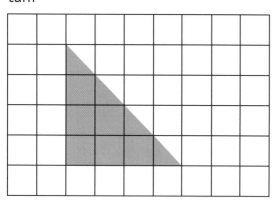 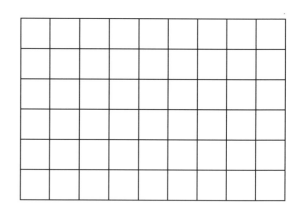

③ flip

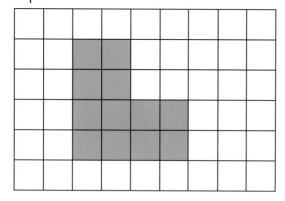 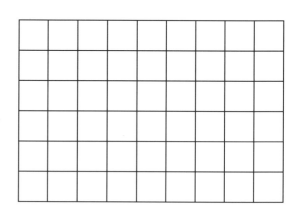

④ turn

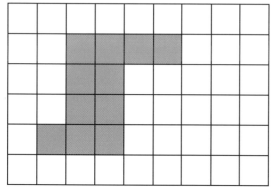 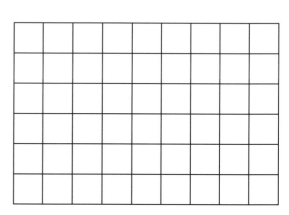

TARGETING HOMEWORK 2 © PASCAL PRESS ISBN 9781925726442

The calendar

April						
Sunday	**Monday**	**Tuesday**	**Wednesday**	**Thursday**	**Friday**	**Saturday**
				1	2 Good Friday	3
4 Easter Sunday	5 Easter Monday	6	7	8	9	10
11	12	13	14	15	16	17
18	19	20	21	22	23	24
25 Anzac Day	26	27	28	29	30	

☐ Special days and public holidays   ☐ School holidays

⑤ What day is the first of April? _____

⑥ What day is the last of April? _____

⑦ How many days are there in April? _____

⑧ What is the date of the last day of school before school holidays? _____

⑨ What is the date of the first day of school after the school holidays? _____

⑩ How many days in April are school days? _____

⑪ What day is Anzac Day? _____

⑫ How many days in April are special days or public holidays? _____

⑬ What was the last day of March? _____

⑭ What date will be the first day of school in May? _____

Score 2 points for each correct answer!   SCORE | **/28** (0-12) (14-22) (24-28)

TERM 4 MATHS

Problem Solving

AC9M2SP01

Draw the shape that comes next in each pattern.

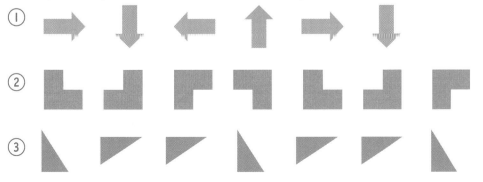

Grammar & Punctuation

AC9E2LA09

Emotion – feeling words

We can use many words to describe our **emotions** or **feelings**. Some emotions feel good. Some feel not so good. But our emotions are not bad – they are what make us human. It is important to recognise our emotions and deal with them in positive ways.

angry annoyed anxious bored brave cheerful confused disappointed embarrassed excited frightened frustrated grumpy guilty happy jealous joyful kind lonely loving nervous proud sad shy silly sorry surprised tired worried

Choose emotion words from the box above to complete these sentences.

① The children were _____ when the circus came to town.

② The boy was _____ that he broke his mother's favourite vase.

③ The girl was _____ when she wasn't chosen for the team.

④ The actor felt _____ when he received the award.

⑤ The new boy felt _____ because he had not made any friends yet.

⑥ The children felt _____ about meeting their new teacher.

⑦ The class was _____ when the work wasn't explained clearly.

⑧ The boy was _____ when the big dog barked at him.

⑨ The parents were _____ when their children were late after school.

⑩ The children were _____ after a long day in the car.

Draw lines to match the feeling adjectives to the feeling nouns.

When I feel ...	The feeling is ...
⑪ happy	anger
⑫ proud	sorrow
⑬ disappointed	excitement
⑭ angry	confusion
⑮ guilty	pride
⑯ sorry	loneliness
⑰ excited	surprise
⑱ surprised	disappointment
⑲ confused	happiness
⑳ lonely	guilt

Score 2 points for each correct answer!

SCORE /40 (0-18) (20-34) (36-40)

TARGETING HOMEWORK 2 © PASCAL PRESS ISBN 9781925726442

Compound words

Compound words are formed by joining two words together to make a new word, like **matchbox** and **butterfly**.

Draw lines to match words that make a compound word.

	First word	Second word		First word	Second word
①	super	mother	⑥	news	light
②	sun	port	⑦	blue	stick
③	air	flower	⑧	candle	times
④	hair	cut	⑨	some	paper
⑤	grand	hero	⑩	moon	berry

Write the two words that have been joined to make these compound words.

⑪ _____ + _____ = mousetrap

⑫ _____ + _____ = lighthouse

⑬ _____ + _____ = rainbow

⑭ _____ + _____ = rattlesnake

⑮ _____ + _____ = schoolwork

⑯ _____ + _____ = spaceship

⑰ _____ + _____ = watermelon

⑱ _____ + _____ = strawberry

⑲ _____ + _____ = teaspoon

⑳ _____ + _____ = brainstorm

Use compound words from this page to complete the sentences.

㉑ When the sun came out, we saw a beautiful _____ in the sky.

㉒ When my _____ came to visit, she spoiled us with treats.

㉓ The aliens arrived in a _____ from outer space.

㉔ If it wasn't for the _____, we wouldn't be able to see at night.

㉕ The _____ sits on the rocky cliffs to warn the ships of danger.

Score 2 points for each correct answer! SCORE /50 0-22 24-44 46-50

Trace the words. Start at the star. Follow the arrows.

The children ate all the strawberries.

AC9E2LA03, AC9E2LA08, AC9E2LY05

Reading & Comprehension

Informative text – Procedure

How to Play Dots and Dashes

Dots and Dashes is an easy game to play for two or more players. All you need is a friend or two, one piece of paper and a pencil each.

The object of the game is to win the most squares.

To set up the game

Draw a grid of dots. You can have any number of dots, but ten rows of ten dots is a good start.

To play

1 Decide who goes first.

2 Take turns to join two dots, either horizontally or vertically. Diagonally is not allowed. The dots must be next to each other.

3 The player who places the fourth line to close a square wins that square and writes their initial inside it.

4 If you win a square, you may continue joining dots until you can't make any more squares.

5 Don't make it easy for your opponents to make squares. In the beginning, it is easy. As the game progresses, it becomes more difficult.

6 The winner is the player who forms the most squares.

Write or tick the correct answer.

① This text is a

☐ **a** poem.   ☐ **b** procedure.   ☐ **c** story.   ☐ **d** non-fiction text.

TARGETING HOMEWORK 2 © PASCAL PRESS ISBN 9781925726442

TERM 4 ENGLISH

② How many people can play?

_____

③ To play the game you need

☐ **a** a pack of cards.

☐ **c** a board and dice.

☐ **b** a football.

☐ **d** paper and pencils.

④ What do you do to set up the game?

_____

⑤ What is the object of the game?

☐ **a** to score goals

☐ **b** to finish first

☐ **c** to make the longest line

☐ **d** to win the most squares

⑥ How do you win a square?

☐ **a** by drawing the last side

☐ **b** by taking it from your opponent

☐ **c** by drawing all the sides at the same time

☐ **d** by colouring it

⑦ The dots you join

☐ **a** can make a diagonal line

☐ **b** can make a horizontal or vertical line

☐ **c** must be next to each other

☐ **d** both b. and c.

⑧ If you make a square by joining two dots

☐ **a** your turn is finished.

☐ **b** you may have another turn.

☐ **c** you are out of the game.

☐ **d** you must go back to the start.

⑨ The winner is the player who

☐ **a** wins the most squares.

☐ **b** has the most turns.

☐ **c** draws the longest line.

☐ **d** goes first.

⑩ How many dots do you need to draw?

☐ **a** 10   ☐ **c** 50

☐ **b** 100   ☐ **d** any number

Score 2 points for each correct answer! **SCORE** **/20** (0-8) (10-14) (16-20)

My Book Review

Title _____

Author _____

Colour stars to show your rating: ☆ ☆ ☆ ☆ ☆

Boring   Great!

Comment _____

_____

Numbers over 100

TERM 4 MATHS

① Circle the numbers you would count if you started at 7 and counted in 10s.

17   87   107   70   173   297   867   779   670   575

② Write the orange numbers above in order from **lowest to highest** (ascending order).

_____, _____, _____, _____, _____, _____, _____, _____, _____, _____

③ Circle the numbers you would count if you started at 28 and counted in 2s.

46   82   120   123   475   876   643   292   587   999

④ Write the orange numbers above in order from **highest to lowest** (descending order).

_____, _____, _____, _____, _____, _____, _____, _____, _____, _____

Write the next number in these counting sequences. Explain how you are counting.

⑤ 263, 266, 269, _____   I am counting **F B** in _____.

⑥ 450, 445, 440, _____   I am counting **F B** in _____.

⑦ 25, 125, 135, _____   I am counting **F B** in _____.

⑧ 569, 469, 369, _____   I am counting **F B** in _____.

⑨ 687, 677, 667, _____   I am counting **F B** in _____.

Complete these counting on sequences.

⑩ 27 [+1] _____ [+2] _____ [+3] _____ [+5] _____ [+10] _____ [+100] _____

⑪ 81 [+1] _____ [+2] _____ [+3] _____ [+5] _____ [+10] _____ [+100] _____

⑫ 134 [+1] _____ [+2] _____ [+3] _____ [+5] _____ [+10] _____ [+100] _____

⑬ 256 [+1] _____ [+2] _____ [+3] _____ [+5] _____ [+10] _____ [+100] _____

Show these numbers on the abacuses.

⑭ 367
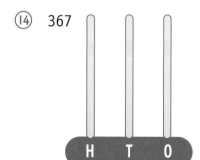

⑮ 640
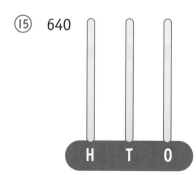

⑯ 209
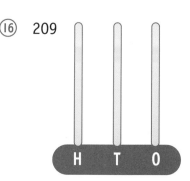

TARGETING HOMEWORK 2 © PASCAL PRESS ISBN 9781925726442

Write the numbers shown on these abacuses.

⑰ 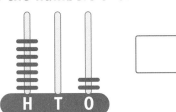 [ ]

⑱ 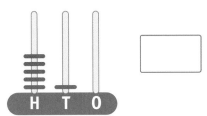 [ ]

Complete this table.

	Blocks	Number	Expanded	H T O
⑲	(blocks shown)		_____ + _____ + _____	____ hundreds ____ tens ____ ones
⑳		654	_____ + _____ + _____	____ hundreds ____ tens ____ ones
㉑			200 + 30 + 5	____ hundreds ____ tens ____ ones
㉒			_____ + _____ + _____	5 hundreds 7 tens 0 ones

TERM 4 MATHS

Partition these numbers in different ways. The first one is done for you.

246	2 hundreds + 4 tens + 6 ones
246	24 tens + 6 ones
246	2 hundreds + 46 ones

㉓	425	
	425	
	425	

㉔	507	
	507	
	507	

TERM 4 MATHS

㉕ The baker baked 12 cookies.
He shared them onto three trays so that each tray had the same number.
How many cookies did he put on each tray?

Draw the cookies on the trays. Complete the division fact.

12 cookies shared onto three trays = _____ cookies on each tray.   **12 ÷ 3 = _____**

㉖ A football player had 10 socks. She folded them into pairs.
How many pairs did she make?

Draw lines to combine the pairs. Complete the division fact.

10 socks divided into pairs = _____ pairs of socks.   **10 ÷ 2 = _____**

Money

Look at these items in the shop. Circle the money you would use to buy each item.

㉗ $1.50

㉘ $5.75

㉙ $7.10

㉚ $4.25

Score 2 points for each correct answer!   SCORE /60   0-28   30-54   56-60

TARGETING HOMEWORK 2 © PASCAL PRESS ISBN 9781925726442

Picture graphs

The children made a picture graph to show what sort of pets they owned.
Some children owned more than one kind of pet. Some children didn't have a pet.

Each 😊 stands for one child.

Dog	😊 😊 😊 😊 😊 😊 😊 😊
Cat	😊 😊 😊 😊 😊
Fish	😊 😊 😊 😊 😊 😊
Guinea pig	😊 😊
Bird	😊 😊 😊 😊
Mouse	😊 😊 😊
Rat	😊
No pet	😊 😊 😊 😊

① What is the most popular pet?

_____

② What is the least popular pet?

_____

③ How many children have a cat?

_____

④ Do more children have cats or dogs?

_____

⑤ How many children have guinea pigs? _____

⑥ Do more children have guinea pigs or mice? _____

⑦ Do more children have birds or guinea pigs? _____

⑧ How many more children have fish than rats? _____

⑨ How many children don't have a pet? _____

⑩ If there are 25 children in the class, how many of them have pets? _____

Score 2 points for each correct answer! **SCORE** **/20** (0-8) (10-14) (16-20)

Problem Solving

AC9M2N06

The baker had 12 cookies ready to pack onto trays.
He wanted the same number of cookies on each tray, but he didn't want any left over.
How many trays could he use, and how many cookies would he put on each tray?

There are six different ways. Can you find them all?

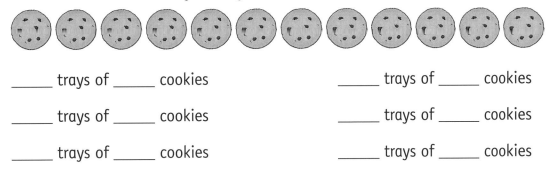

_____ trays of _____ cookies   _____ trays of _____ cookies

_____ trays of _____ cookies   _____ trays of _____ cookies

_____ trays of _____ cookies   _____ trays of _____ cookies

Grammar & Punctuation

AC9E2LA09

Emotion – feeling words

We can use many words to describe our **emotions** or **feelings**. Some emotions feel good. Some feel not so good. But our emotions are not bad – they are what make us human. It is important to recognise our emotions and deal with them in positive ways.

angry annoyed anxious bored brave cheerful confused disappointed
embarrassed excited frightened frustrated grumpy guilty happy jealous joyful
kind lonely loving nervous proud sad shy silly sorry surprised tired worried

Draw a tick in the box for the good feelings and a cross for the not-so-good feelings.

1. ☐ happy
2. ☐ brave
3. ☐ proud
4. ☐ guilty
5. ☐ kind
6. ☐ embarrassed
7. ☐ sorry

8. ☐ tired
9. ☐ jealous
10. ☐ loving
11. ☐ angry
12. ☐ lonely
13. ☐ sad
14. ☐ bored

15. ☐ shy
16. ☐ disappointed
17. ☐ frightened
18. ☐ cheerful
19. ☐ excited
20. ☐ anxious
21. ☐ annoyed

22. ☐ surprised
23. ☐ confused
24. ☐ grumpy
25. ☐ joyful
26. ☐ nervous
27. ☐ silly
28. ☐ worried

29–39 Circle the 11 words that tell you about feelings in this story.

The day was hot, and the group had been walking for a long time. They were exhausted. The sun was starting to go down and they were worried that they wouldn't find somewhere to sleep before nightfall.

Many in the group began to grumble. Some of them were just disappointed, but Paige was cross. Dustin had told them proudly that he knew the way. Now that they were lost, Dustin was embarrassed.

Sarah told him not to worry, that they would find somewhere soon. Paige was doubtful and she wasn't ready to forgive him.

Soon Brand called out excitedly, "Look, there's a camping spot."

Dustin was relieved. "This is the camping spot we were looking for," he said. "We weren't lost after all."

Write a word that tells how they are feeling now.

40. Dustin _____
41. Sarah _____

42. Paige _____
43. Everyone _____

Score 2 points for each correct answer!

SCORE /86   (0-40)   (42-80)   (82-86)

TARGETING HOMEWORK 2 © PASCAL PRESS ISBN 9781925726442

TERM 4 ENGLISH

Compound words

Compound words are formed by joining two words together to make a new word, like **superhero** and **teaspoon**.

Start with the word in the middle. Make compound words by joining it to the other words. Write the compound words.

less	light
gaze	**star**	ship
like		fish
dust	fruit

①	⑤
②	⑥
③	⑦
④	⑧

ball	bag
work	**hand**	shake
book		write
over	stand

⑨	⑬
⑩	⑭
⑪	⑮
⑫	⑯

place	fighter
works	**fire**	ball
break		storm
hose	box

⑰	㉑
⑱	㉒
⑲	㉓
⑳	㉔

play	plane
head	**air**	port
mail		craft
brush	sick

㉕	㉙
㉖	㉚
㉗	㉛
㉘	㉜

TERM 4 ENGLISH

Score 2 points for each correct answer!

SCORE

/64   0-30   32-58   60-64

Trace the words. Start at the star. Follow the arrows.

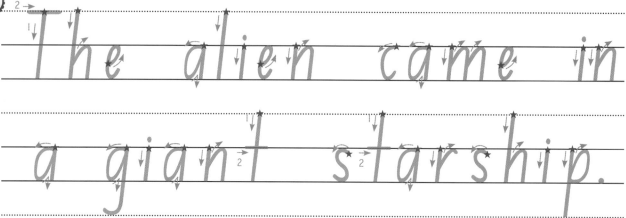

The alien came in

a giant starship.

TERM 4 ENGLISH

Reading & Comprehension

AC9E2LA03, AC9E2LA08, AC9E2LY03, AC9E2LY05

Persuasive text – Letter

Please Forgive Me

Illustrator: Paul Lennon

Dear Bear family,

I am sorry I went into your house without asking. I know it wasn't the right thing to do, but I couldn't help myself. You see, I had been lost in the forest for days and I was very hungry. I had not had anything to eat – only a few berries. When I smelled your porridge, it smelled so good, I just had to have some.

I didn't mean to eat all of Baby Bear's porridge. I really didn't. And I didn't mean to break his chair. I was so tired after being lost in the forest that I fell asleep on his bed.

When you came home, I woke up. I was frightened so I ran away. I didn't want to be put in jail. I am really sorry. I will make you some more porridge and fix Baby Bear's chair if you let me.

Please forgive me,
Goldilocks

Write or tick the correct answer.

① This text is a

☐ **a** poem. ☐ **b** narrative. ☐ **c** letter. ☐ **d** report.

② The purpose of the text is to

☐ **a** give information.

☐ **b** make the bears laugh.

☐ **c** entertain.

☐ **d** persuade.

③ Who is the letter written to?

☐ **a** Goldilocks   ☐ **c** Baby Bear

☐ **b** The Bear family   ☐ **d** The police

④ What does Goldilocks want the Bear family to do?

☐ **a** Forgive her.

☐ **b** Write her a letter.

☐ **c** Forget what she did.

☐ **d** Tell the police.

⑤ Why did Goldilocks go into the Bears' house?

☐ **a** because she was naughty

☐ **b** because she was hungry

☐ **c** because she didn't like bears

☐ **d** because the bears invited her

⑥ How did Goldilocks feel when the Bears came home?

☐ **a** frightened   ☐ **c** hungry

☐ **b** tired   ☐ **d** sorry

⑦ How did Goldilocks feel when she wrote the letter?

☐ **a** sad   ☐ **c** frightened

☐ **b** sorry   ☐ **d** happy

⑧ Which of these things did Goldilocks say that she would do?

☐ **a** Make some honey for them.

☐ **b** Fix Baby Bear's chair.

☐ **c** Go to jail.

☐ **d** Make the beds.

⑨ Do you think the Bear family will forgive Goldilocks?

☐ **a** yes   ☐ **b** no

⑩ Why?

_____

_____

TERM 4 ENGLISH

Score 2 points for each correct answer!   **SCORE**   **/20**   (0-8)   (10-14)   (16-20)

My Book Review

Title _____

Author _____

Colour stars to show your rating.   ☆ ☆ ☆ ☆ ☆

Boring   Great!

Comment _____

_____

Number & Algebra

AC9M2N01, AC9M2N03, AC9M2N04, AC9M2N05, AC9M2A01

Numbers over 100

Write the missing numbers in these sequences.

① 257, 357, 457, _____, _____, _____, _____, _____

② 321, 331, 341, _____, _____, _____, _____, _____

③ 998, 988, 978, _____, _____, _____, _____, _____

④ 127, 126, 125, _____, _____, _____, _____, _____

⑤ 505, 510, 515, _____, _____, _____, _____, _____

Complete this table.

	100 less	10 less	1 less		1 more	10 more	100 more
⑥				**620**			
⑦				**899**			
⑧				**117**			
⑨				**305**			

Arrange these 3 digits to make 6 numbers.
Write them in order from smallest to largest.

⑩ **8 5 9** _____, _____, _____, _____, _____, _____

⑪ **6 2 0** _____, _____, _____, _____, _____, _____

⑫ **3 9 7** _____, _____, _____, _____, _____, _____

Read these number stories. Draw the picture.
Circle + or – to show if it is addition or subtraction. Then write the number fact.

⑬ A farmer had 8 sheep. He bought 7 more sheep.
How many sheep does he have altogether?

+ – _____

⑭ Tema had 16 marbles. He gave 6 to Sarah.
How many marbles does he have now?

+ – _____

TARGETING HOMEWORK 2 © PASCAL PRESS ISBN 9781925726442

⑮ Sam had $7 in his money box. He spent $3.
How much money does Sam have left?

+ − _____

⑯ Zane invited 14 friends to his party.
Three of his friends couldn't come.
How many friends came to his party?

+ − _____

Look at these arrays.
Write the two multiplication facts.

⑰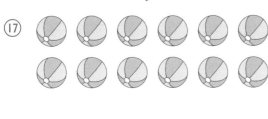

_____

_____

⑱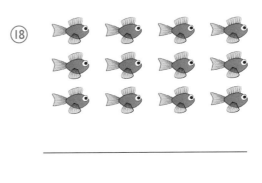

_____

_____

⑲ There were 9 flowers and 3 vases.
Sam put an equal number of flowers into each vase.
How many flowers did he put in each vase?
Draw the flowers. Write the division fact.

_____

Halves, quarters and eighths

Write halves, quarters or eighths for each picture.

⑳ 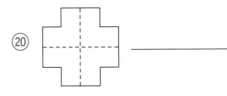 _____

㉑  _____

㉒  _____

㉓ 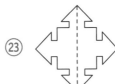 _____

㉔ _____

㉕  _____

There are 16 toy cars in the box.

26 Sam and Jamie share the cars to have half each. How many cars do they have?
Draw pictures to show your answers.

Sam	Jamie

27 How many each? _____

28 Sam, Jamie, Zane and Sarah share the cars equally. How many do they have each?
Draw pictures to show your answers.

Sam	Jamie	Zane	Sarah

29 How many each? _____

30 Sam, Jamie, Zane and Sarah each work with a friend.
They share the toys so that they all have the same number.
How many do they have? Draw pictures to show your answers.

Sam	Friend	Jamie	Friend	Zane	Friend	Sarah	Friend

31 How many each? _____

32 Circle the part that is biggest.

    a one half   **b** one quarter   **c** one eighth

Score 2 points
for each
correct answer!

SCORE **/64**

TARGETING HOMEWORK 2 © PASCAL PRESS ISBN 9781925726442

Collecting data

Everyone in Tema's class was surveyed to find out how they came to school most days. The children used tally marks to collect the information:

Car ‖‖ ‖‖ ‖	Walk ‖‖ ‖‖‖‖	Bicycle ‖‖‖‖	Bus ‖‖

① Show the information in a picture graph where 😊 stands for one child.

Car	

② Now show the same information in the table at the right by colouring one box for each child.

③ Write a question for the survey.

_____

_____

④ Write two things you found out from the survey.

_____

_____

12				
11				
10				
9				
8				
7				
6				
5				
4				
3				
2				
1				
	Car	Walk	Bicycle	Bus

Score 2 points for each correct answer!

SCORE /8   (0-2)   (4-6)   (8)

Problem Solving

AC9M2M02, AC9M2ST01, AC9M2ST02

Look at these spinners.

A 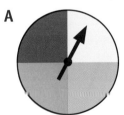   B 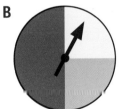   C 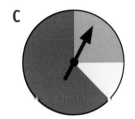   D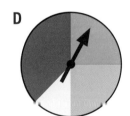

① Which spinner gives you the best chance of spinning red? _____

② If you definitely don't want to spin blue, which spinner should you choose? _____

③ Which spinner gives you an equal chance of spinning red, yellow, blue or green? _____

Grammar & Punctuation

ask careful chuckle depart difficult everyone future happy old shout tall

Write a synonym for the underlined word. Choose words from the box above.

① _____ Although the boy did his best, he thought the work was <u>hard</u>.

② _____ The teacher was <u>pleased</u> with the way the children worked.

③ _____ The <u>elderly</u> man used a stick to help him walk.

④ _____ Everyone said 'goodbye' when it was time to <u>leave</u>.

⑤ _____ You must not <u>yell</u> in the classroom.

Write an antonym for the underlined word. Choose words from the box above.

⑥ _____ The girl was surprised when <u>no one</u> came to the party.

⑦ _____ It was Kalim's turn to <u>answer</u> the questions.

⑧ _____ Kali was very <u>careless</u> with her work.

⑨ _____ The <u>short</u> man is the first in line.

⑩ _____ It is interesting to talk about the <u>past</u>.

Choose feeling words from the box to complete the sentences.

angry annoyed anxious bored brave cheerful confused disappointed embarrassed excited frightened frustrated grumpy guilty happy jealous joyful kind lonely loving nervous proud sad shy silly sorry surprised tired worried

⑪ The dog was _____ by the loud thunder.

⑫ Evan was _____ when his friend was chosen to play instead of him.

⑬ Zoe was _____ when she couldn't go outside to play.

⑭ The little boy was _____ when he couldn't open the door.

⑮ The toddler was _____ when he was woken up too soon.

⑯ The shopkeeper was _____ when a display of apples was knocked over.

⑰ Children sometimes feel _____ when they meet new people.

Score 2 points for each correct answer! **SCORE** **/34** (0-14) (16-28) (30-34)

TARGETING HOMEWORK 2 © PASCAL PRESS ISBN 9781925726442

Syllables

Read these words. Add / to show the syllable breaks.

① paper   ④ carrot   ⑦ button   ⑨ pencil

② because   ⑤ butter   ⑧ manner   ⑩ planet

③ open   ⑥ clever

Read the words. In the box, write how many syllables the word has.

⑪ ☐ somersault   ⑯ ☐ cartwheel   ㉑ ☐ basketball

⑫ ☐ soccer   ⑰ ☐ tennis   ㉒ ☐ swim

⑬ ☐ run   ⑱ ☐ gallop   ㉓ ☐ flutter

⑭ ☐ hop   ⑲ ☐ flower   ㉔ ☐ vegetable

⑮ ☐ potato   ⑳ ☐ steak   ㉕ ☐ gravy

Draw lines to match words that make a compound word.

First Word	Second Word		First Word	Second Word
㉖ suit	coat		㉛ lap	dog
㉗ note	case		㉜ book	mark
㉘ rain	fish		㉝ ring	man
㉙ ear	book		㉞ snow	top
㉚ cat	ring		㉟ hot	side

Choose compound words from the activity above to complete the sentences.

㊱ The boy got wet on the way home because he forgot his _____.

㊲ After it snowed, the children made a _____ in the park.

㊳ The girl ate a _____ with tomato sauce at the show.

㊴ The children did their coding at home on their _____ computers.

㊵ I packed my _____, ready to go on holidays.

㊶ I wrote some ideas in my _____ so I wouldn't forget them.

Score 2 points for each correct answer! SCORE /82

Number & Algebra

| 507 | 750 | 625 | 978 | 432 | 197 | 864 | 302 | 420 | 345 |

① Look at the numbers in the box. Circle the largest number. Cross the smallest number.

② Arrange the numbers in the box in order from **smallest to largest** (ascending order).

_____, _____, _____, _____, _____, _____, _____, _____, _____, _____.

Write the numbers shown on these abacuses.

③ 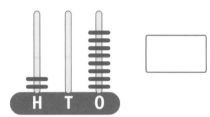 ☐

④ 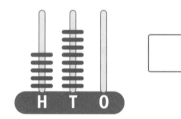 ☐

Expand these numbers.

⑤ 851 = _____ + _____ + ___ or ___ hundreds, ___ tens, ___ one

⑥ 597 = _____ + _____ + ___ or ___ hundreds, ___ tens, ___ ones

⑦ 230 = _____ + _____ + ___ or ___ hundreds, ___ tens, ___ ones

⑧ 409 = _____ + _____ + ___ or ___ hundreds, ___ tens, ___ ones

Look at these pictures. Circle the matching number sentence.

⑨ ★★★★★
★★★★★

$2 + 5 = 7$ $10 - 2 = 8$ $2 \times 5 = 10$

⑪

$8 + 4 = 12$ $8 - 4 = 4$ $2 \times 4 = 8$

⑩

$8 \div 4 = 2$ $4 + 2 = 6$ $8 - 4 = 4$

⑫

$6 - 4 = 2$ $2 \times 6 = 12$ $6 + 4 = 10$

Draw lines to divide these shapes.

⑬ halves

⑭ quarters

⑮ eighths

Measurement & Space

① How many blocks to you need to add to make the toy truck balance? _____

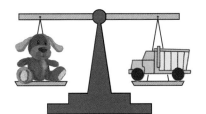  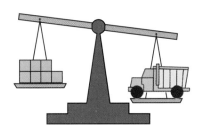

Colour the 3D shapes to match.

② cube: blue   ④ sphere: red   ⑥ cylinder: green

③ cone: yellow   ⑤ pyramid: purple   ⑦ rectangular prism: orange

Look at these pairs of pictures. Circle the word that tells how they have moved.

⑧

slide   flip   turn

⑨

slide   flip   turn

⑩

slide   flip   turn

Score 2 points for each correct answer! SCORE **/20** (0-8) (10-14) (16-20)

Statistics

The children were comparing how many runs they made in their cricket match. Tema scored 13. Sasha scored 18. Li scored 7 and Zayne was out for a duck (0).

① Use tallies to show their runs.

Tema	Sasha	Li	Zayne

Write two questions you could ask about this information. Write the answers too.

② _____

_____

③ _____

_____

Score 2 points for each correct answer! SCORE **/6** (0) (2-4) (6)

MY READING LIST

Name: _____

_____

	Title	Author	Rating	Date
1			☆☆☆☆☆	
2			☆☆☆☆☆	
3			☆☆☆☆☆	
4			☆☆☆☆☆	
5			☆☆☆☆☆	
6			☆☆☆☆☆	
7			☆☆☆☆☆	
8			☆☆☆☆☆	
9			☆☆☆☆☆	
10			☆☆☆☆☆	
11			☆☆☆☆☆	
12			☆☆☆☆☆	
13			☆☆☆☆☆	
14			☆☆☆☆☆	
15			☆☆☆☆☆	
16			☆☆☆☆☆	
17			☆☆☆☆☆	
18			☆☆☆☆☆	
19			☆☆☆☆☆	
20			☆☆☆☆☆	
21			☆☆☆☆☆	
22			☆☆☆☆☆	
23			☆☆☆☆☆	
24			☆☆☆☆☆	
25			☆☆☆☆☆	
26			☆☆☆☆☆	
27			☆☆☆☆☆	
28			☆☆☆☆☆	
29			☆☆☆☆☆	
30			☆☆☆☆☆	
31			☆☆☆☆☆	
32			☆☆☆☆☆	

TARGETING HOMEWORK 2 © PASCAL PRESS ISBN 9781925726442

Unit 1 English: Grammar & Punctuation

1 ✗
2 S
3 ✗
4 ✗
5 S
6 ✗
7 S
8 ✗
9 The girl in the green shirt came first in the race.
10 After the rain stopped, the sun came out.
11 Before you go home, make sure you have everything you need.
12 We went to the beach for our holidays.
13–16 Answers will vary; sample answers provided. Each sentence should have a verb.
13 The red car raced down the road.
14 The big brown horse was friendly.
15 The frightened child hid under the bed.
16 The blue balloon floated free above the crowds.
17 The enormous crocodile was sleeping on the river bank.
18 chases
19 grows
20 dance
21 flies

Unit 1 English: Phonic Knowledge & Spelling

1 watching, watched
2 cracking, cracked
3 wishing, wished
4 looking, looked
5 cape
6 rode
7 mane
8 note
9 ride
10 cube
11 kite
12 huge
13 mane
14 kite
15 home
16 time
17 huge
18 rid
19 can
20 not
21 mope
22 cub

Unit 1 English: Reading & Comprehension

1 c. the circus
2 b. Tinks
3 in the front row
4 a. the lion tamer
5 c. the place where circus acts are performed
6 a. They were closer.
7 the lions
8 c. They were already being used.
9 a. The lions roared at her.
10 Answers will vary.

Unit 2 MATHS: Number & Algebra

1 2, 4, 6, 8, 10, 12, 14, 16
2 18, 22, 26, 28, 30, 34, F
3 64, 66, 68, 70, 74, 76, 78, F
4 48, 44, 42, 40, 36, 34, 32, B
5 84, 82, 80, 78, 76, 72, 70, B
6 17, 27, 56, 65, 72

7 16, 60, 61, 63, 96
8 99, 96, 69, 66, 16
9 85, 81, 58, 55, 18
10 95, 9
11 5 + 4 = 9, 4 + 5 = 9
12 6 + 2 = 8, 2 + 6 = 8
13 4 + 3 = 7, 3 + 4 = 7
14 1 + 5 = 6, 5 + 1 = 6
15 8
16 5, 6 + 5 = 11
17 4, 5 + 4 = 9
18 5, 5 + 5 = 10
19 3, 4 + 3 = 7

Unit 2 MATHS: Measurement & Space

1 7 coins
2 2 coins
3 8 coins
4 1 coin
5 3 coins or 3.5 coins
6 9 coins
7 15 coins
8 10 coins
9 blue, straight
10 green straight and curved
11 yellow, curved
12 green, curved and straight
13 blue, straight
14 yellow, curved

Unit 2 MATHS: Problem Solving

1 Answers will vary.
2 Answers will vary.

Unit 3 English: Grammar & Punctuation

1 Q
2 Q
3 Q
4 Q
5 S
6 S
7 Q
8 S
9 Q
10–15 Answers will vary; sample answers provided. Each question should have a verb and a question mark at the end.
10 Who went to the beach on the weekend?
11 What did the children do on the weekend?
12 Where did the children go on the weekend?
13 When did the children go to the beach?
14 Why did the children go to the beach?
15 How did the children get to the beach?

ANSWERS

Unit 3 English: Phonic Knowledge & Spelling

1	looking	7	happy	13	fried
2	painted	8	tall	14	grey
3	climbing	9	height	15	snail
4	planted	10	key	16	equal
5	packed	11	egg	17	grey
6	guessed	12	head	18	key

Unit 3 English: Reading & Comprehension

1 b. insects
2 b. invertebrates
3 a. insects
4 a. about
5 c. mammals
6 invertebrates
7 c. fish
8 d. purple
9 c. amphibians
10 a. reptiles

Unit 4 MATHS: Number & Algebra

1

1	2	3	4	5	6	7	8	9	10
11	12	13	14	15	16	17	18	19	20
21	22	23	24	25	26	27	28	29	30
31	32	33	34	35	36	37	38	39	40
41	42	43	44	45	46	47	48	49	50
51	52	53	54	55	56	57	58	59	60
61	62	63	64	65	66	67	68	69	70
71	72	73	74	75	76	77	78	79	80
81	82	83	84	85	86	87	88	89	90
91	92	93	94	95	96	97	98	99	100

2 21, 24, 27, 33, 36, 42. F
3 51, 48, 45, 42, 36, 33, 30. B
4 72, 78, 81, 87, 90, 93, 96. F
5 75, 72, 69, 66, 57, 54, 48. B
6 35
7 56
8 20
9 75
10 42
11 96
12 13, 18, 27, 31, 68, 81, 86, 88
13 92, 65, 54, 42, 38, 29, 18, 9
14 30
15 40
16 60
17 50
18 8 + 2 = 10
19 10 − 2 = 8
20 7 + 3 = 10
21 10 − 3 = 7
22 5 + 2 = 7
23 $5 + $4 = $9
24 10 − 3 = 7
25 9 − 5 = 4

Unit 4 MATHS: Measurement & Space

1 Answers will vary, but paths should pass the hat shop.
2 Answers will vary; e.g. mall
3 Answers will vary; e.g. book shop
4 Answers will vary; e.g. hat shop
5 Answers will vary; e.g. pedestrian crossing
6 Answers will vary; e.g. park
7 Answers will vary; e.g. pedestrian crossing
8 right
9 Answers will vary; e.g. have a swim, play in the playground, play in the sand, go to the amusement hall, go to the movies.
10 4 o'clock
11 half past 4
12 half past 8
13 10 o'clock

Unit 4 MATHS: Problem Solving

1 Beth   2 2 o'clock

Unit 5 English: Grammar & Punctuation

1	C	9	R
2	R	10	C
3	R	11	Open the door.
4	R	12	Turn off the light.
5	C	13	Help me wash the car.
6	C	14	Take the bin outside.
7	R	15	Take the dog for a walk.
8	C		

Unit 5 English: Phonic Knowledge & Spelling

1	taping, taped	6	copying, copied	12	pit
2	liking, liked	7	tidying, tidied	13	tray
3	smiling, smiled	8	frying, fried	14	not
4	changing, changed	9	fin	15	shone
5	drying, dried	10	eight	16	now
		11	bigger	17	rod
				18	down

Unit 5 English: Reading & Comprehension

1 b. He went to circus school.
2 c. that Colin wasn't very good at circus tricks.
3 d. secret music
4 c. He played music.
5 a. He wore a special music suit.
6 d. all of the above
7 a. yes
8 a. surprised
9 b. proud
10 a. at the beginning of the show

TARGETING HOMEWORK 2 © PASCAL PRESS ISBN 9781925726442

Unit 6 MATHS: Number & Algebra

1 5, 10, 15, 20, 25, 30, 35, 40, 45, 50, 55, 60, 65, 70

2

5	10	15	20	25
30	35	40	45	50
55	60	65	70	75
80	85	90	95	100

3 15, 20, 25, 30, 40, 45, 50. F
4 45, 35, 30, 25, 20, 10, 5. B
5 75, 70, 65, 60, 50, 45, 40. B

6 14
7 38
8 21
9 6 + 4 = 10
10 4 + 6 = 10
11 10 – 6 = 4
12 10 – 4 = 6
13 3 + 5 = 8
14 5 + 3 = 8

15 8 – 5 = 3
16 8 – 3 = 5
17 7, 8, 9
18 9, 10
19 8, 7
20 7, 6, 5
21 $2 is green.
22 5c is red.
23 50c is ticked.

24 5c is crossed.
25 five 10c coins
26 four 5c coins
27 two $1 coins
28 five 20c coins
29 two 5c coins
30 four 50c coins
31 $9

Unit 6 MATHS: Statistics

1 Group 3
2 Group 1
3 Group 2
4 Group 4
5 Group 4, no
6 Group 2, supreme
7 Group 1, crows
8 Group 3, hockey
9 Group 1, 2
10 Group 2, 4
11 Group 4, 21
12 Group 2 and Group 3

Unit 6 MATHS: Problem Solving

$2, 20c, 10c, 5c

Unit 7 Grammar and Punctuation

1 For breakfast, I had eggs, bacon, mushroom, tomatoes and toast.
2 Sam invited Mark, Tema, Zayne, Jess and Sarah to his party.
3 I used paper, cardboard, glue and paint to make my toy boat.
4 The shop was selling books, cards, wrapping paper and other gifts.
5–9 Answers will vary; sample answers provided. Each sentence should have a verb.
5 Sam took paper, pencils, a scrapbook and sticky tape.
6 Sarah took a hat, gloves, a mask, sunglasses and insect spray.
7 Tema took a book, a torch and a pillow.
8 Jess took a butterfly net, a magnifying glass, tweezers and two notebooks.
9 Zayne took goggles, sunscreen, a rashie and flippers.

Unit 7 English: Phonic Knowledge & Spelling

1 tipping, tipped
2 robbing, robbed
3 grabbing, grabbed
4 jogging, jogged
5 clapped
6 planning
7 skipped
8 hopping
9 ✗
10 ✓
11 ✓
12 ✗
13 ✓
14 ✓
15 ✓
16 ✗
17 ✓
18 ✗
19 ✓
20 ✗
21 music
22 huge
23 cute

Unit 7 English: Reading & Comprehension

1 c. He had a beard.
2 a. birds.
3 d. 8
4 b. larks
5 c. untamed and scruffy
6 feared
7 Wren
8 a. surprised
9 a. It is silly.
10 c. to make us laugh

Unit 8 MATHS: Number & Algebra

2, 3, 5, 7, 9

1	2	3	4	5	6	7	8	9	10
11	12	13	14	15	16	17	18	19	20
21	22	23	24	25	26	27	28	29	30
31	32	33	34	35	36	37	38	39	40
41	42	43	44	45	46	47	48	49	50
51	52	53	54	55	56	57	58	59	60
61	62	63	64	65	66	67	68	69	70
71	72	73	74	75	76	77	78	79	80
81	82	83	84	85	86	87	88	89	90
91	92	93	94	95	96	97	98	99	100

1 10, 20, 30, 40, 50, 60, 70, 80, 90, 100
4 7, 17, 27, 37, 47, 57, 67, 77, 87, 97
6 5, 15, 25, 35, 45, 55, 65, 75, 85, 95
8 2, 12, 22, 32, 42, 52, 62, 72, 82, 92
10 8, 18, 28, 38, 48, 58, 68, 78, 88, 98
11 62
12 43
13 26
14–18 Answers will vary. 2 addition and 2 subtraction facts to 10, matching the colours of the sheep.
19 16, 17, 18
20 13, 14
21 3 + 3 = 6
22 4 + 4 = 8
23 5 + 5 = 10
24 6 + 6 = 12
25 10 + 4 = 14
26 12 – 3 = 9
27 Answers will vary. For example: Five children were playing a game. Three more children came to play. How many children are playing now?
28 ✓
29 ✓

ANSWERS

30 ✗
31 ✗
32 ✓
33 ✓

34 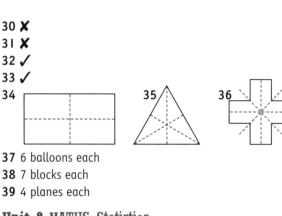 35 36

37 6 balloons each
38 7 blocks each
39 4 planes each

Unit 8 MATHS: Statistics

1 vanilla ||, chocolate ||||, strawberry |, mango |||, choc-mint |
2 What is your favourite ice-cream flavour?
3 Sample answer:
 My friends like chocolate ice-cream the most.

Unit 8 MATHS: Problem Solving

1 2
2 Nala

TERM 1 REVIEW

Term 1 English: Grammar & Punctuation

1 ✗
2 S
3 S
4 S
5 ✗
6–8 Answers will vary; sample answers provided. Each question should have a verb and a question mark at the end.
6 Who won the soccer match on Friday?
7 What did the team play on Friday?
8 When did the team play soccer?
9 C
10 R
11 R
12 C
13 I packed my shirts, shorts, socks, underwear and pyjamas into my bag.
14 Sam invited Sarah, Zayne, Tema and Jake to his birthday party.
15 At the farm, Sam saw horses, cows, sheep, goats and dogs.
16 ate
17 sang
18 wrote
19 washed
20 laid

Term 1 English: Phonic Knowledge & Spelling

1 looking	9 kit	17 tail
2 baked	10 apple	18 home
3 tipped	11 rid	19 tube
4 waving	12 us	20 play
5 washed	13 grey	21 peel
6 cap	14 top	22 side
7 cube	15 meat	23 tight
8 hope	16 music	

Term 1 MATHS: Number & Algebra

1 66, 68, 70, 74, 76, 78. F, 2s
2 55, 65, 70, 75, 80, 90, 95. F, 5s
3 70, 60, 50, 40, 30, 10. B, 10s
4 39, 40, 42, 44, 45, 46, 47. F, 1s
5 17, 47, 57, 67, 77, 97. F, 10s
6 74, 72, 68, 66, 64, 62. B, 2s
7 76, 52, 89
8 25, 36, 15
9 87
10 43
11 $2 + 6 = 8$
12 $6 + 2 = 8$
13 $8 - 2 = 6$
14 $8 - 6 = 2$
15 $4 + 3 = 7$
16 $3 + 4 = 7$
17 $7 - 4 = 3$
18 $7 - 3 = 4$
19 70c
20 50c
21 $10

Term 1 MATHS: Measurement & Space

1 2 3

4 3 o'clock
5 half past 8
6 half past 1
7 12 o'clock

Unit 9 English: Grammar & Punctuation

1 girl, seat, tree
2 dog, bone, house
3 bird, worm, ground
4 kangaroo, fence, grass, paddock
5 little, wooden, shady
6 hungry, dry, old
7 brown, long, wet
8 big, high, long, green
9 Answers will vary.
10 Answers will vary.
11 unhappy/sad
12 full
13 light
14 short
15 closed

Unit 9 English: Phonic Knowledge & Spelling

1–10 Some questions may have more than one correct answer.

1 fly	6 gown	11 lady
2 movie	7 sunny	12 brown
3 toe	8 blow	13 blow
4 cow	9 glue	14 pie
5 moon	10 shoe	15 shook

Unit 9 English: Reading & Comprehension

1 c. voices
2 b. monsters
3 surprised
4 c. They didn't make a sound.
5 shocked
6 d. They stared.
7 b. It was empty, so they moved in.
8 b. excited
9 b. We want to be a circus troupe too!
10 Answers will vary.

Unit 10 MATHS: Number & Algebra

1 1, 2, 3, 4, 5, 6, 7, 8, 9, 10
2 10, 20, 30, 40, 50, 60, 70, 80, 90, 100
3 100, 200, 300, 400, 500, 600, 700, 800, 900, 1000
4 37, 47, 57, 77, 87, 97
5 137, 147, 157, 177, 187, 197
6 20, 25, 30, 40, 45, 50
7 120, 125, 130, 140, 145, 150
8 250, 260, 270, 290, 300, 310
9 4
10 34
11 134
12 7 ones
13 2 tens, 7 ones
14 1 hundred, 2 tens, 7 ones
15 1 hundred, 4 tens, 2 ones = 142
16 2 hundreds, 1 ten, 4 ones = 214

17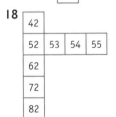
19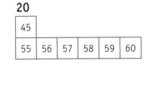

18

20

21 2
22 5
23 10
24 10

Unit 10 MATHS: Measurement & Space

1 square, rectangle, triangle, kite, rhombus
2 circle
3 triangle
4 square, rhombus
5 rectangle, kite
6 4
7 3
8 0
9 4
10 4

Unit 10 MATHS: Problem Solving

26

Unit 11 English: Grammar & Punctuation

1 thought
2 memory
3 reason
4 friendship
5 anger
6 dream
7 C
8 A
9 A
10 C
11 A
12 C
13 A
14 C
15 A
16–20 Answers may vary; sample answers provided.
16 quickly
17 secretly
18 carefully
19 slowly
20 happily

Unit 11 English: Phonic Knowledge & Spelling

1–10 Some questions may have more than one correct answer.

1 astronaut
2 toy
3 cloud
4 soil
5 destroy
6 mouth
7 loud
8 voice
9 cause
10 join
11 you
12 aunt
13 about
14 toll
15 oink

Unit 11 English: Reading & Comprehension

1 b. wasps
2 d. pelicans
3 c. iguanas
4 a. herbivores
5 c. ants
6 a. tortoises
7 a. bearded dragons
8 a. plants
9 c. birds
10 d. cricket

Unit 12 MATHS: Number & Algebra

1 1, 11, 21, 31, 41, 51, 61, 71, 81, 91
2 1, 101, 201, 301, 401, 501, 601, 701, 801, 901
3 10, 110, 210, 310, 410, 510, 610, 710, 810, 910
4 104, 105, 106, 107, 108
5 108, 110, 112, 114, 116
6 120, 125, 130, 135, 140
7 140, 150, 160, 170, 180
8 324, 325, 326, 327, 328
9 528, 530, 532, 534, 536
10 503, 603, 703, 803, 903
11 231
12 123
13 801
14 921
15 Each plate should have 3 apples.

ANSWERS

16 2

17 3

18 6

19 6

20 6

21 Each pen should have 4 sheep.

22 2

23 4

24 8

25 8

26 8

27 Each bowl should have 3 fish.

28 3

29 3

30 9

31 9

32 9

33 Each hoop should have 2 balls.

34 3

35 2

36 6

37 6

38 6

39 8

Unit 12 MATHS: Measurement & Space

1–9
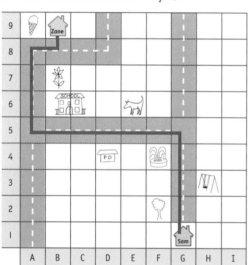

10 Go up 4.
Turn left. Go left 6.
Turn right. Go up 3.
Turn right. Go 1.
Turn left into Zane's house.

11 quarter past 4

12 quarter past 8

13 quarter past 10

14 quarter past 11

15
16

17
18

19   20

Unit 12 MATHS: Problem Solving

1 35

2 16

Unit 13 English: Grammar & Punctuation

1 Ms Pan

2 Rex

3 Saturday

4 Tema

5 Gold Coast, Queensland

6 Canberra, Australia

7 little red riding hood
Little Red Riding Hood

8 the butterfly and the bee
The Butterfly and the Bee

9 snakes and lizards
Snakes and Lizards

10 teacher, one who teaches

11 driver, one who drives

12 learner, one who learns

13 baker, one who bakes

14 speaker, one who speaks

Unit 13 English: Phonic Knowledge & Spelling

1–10 Some questions may have more than one correct answer.

1 shirt

2 calf

3 turtle

4 door

5 water

6 letter

7 Saturday

8 torch

9 fir

10 craft

11 shark

12 torch

13 war

14 board

15 first

Unit 13 English: Reading & Comprehension

1 d. recipe

2 b. make fruit skewers.

3 a. wash the fruit.

4 a. Grow the fruit.

5 Answers will vary – 3 fruits.

6 bite-sized

7 b. carrot

8 a. healthy

9 c. grapes

10 a. watermelon

Unit 14 MATHS: Number & Algebra

1 213, 214, 215, 216, 218, 219

2 372, 371, 370, 367, 366

3 45, 50, 55, 60, 70, 75

4 50, 52, 54, 56, 58, 60

5 487, 587, 687, 787, 987

6 3 hundreds, 5 tens, 4 ones = 354

7 5 hundreds, 2 tens, 6 ones = 526

8 2 hundreds, 5 tens, 4 ones = 254

9 1 hundred, 2 tens, 7 ones = 127

10 865

11 800

12 167

13 73

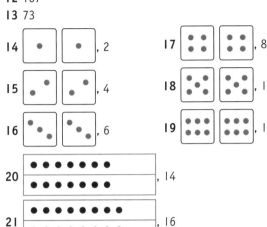

14 , 2

15 , 4

16 , 6

17 , 8

18 , 10

19 , 12

20 , 14

21 , 16

22 , 18

23 , 20

24 green

25 pink

26 $25

27 $50

28 $100

29 $250

30 10

31 20

32 5

33 10

Unit 14 MATHS: Statistics

1 Sheep ⃀⃀⃀⃀⃀ |, 6. Goats ||||, 4

2 Sheep ⃀⃀⃀⃀⃀, 5. Goats ⃀⃀⃀⃀⃀, 5

3 Sheep |||, 3. Goats ⃀⃀⃀⃀⃀ |||, 8

4 Sheep ||||, 4. Goats ⃀⃀⃀⃀⃀ ||, 7

5

	Paddock 1		Paddock 2		Paddock 3		Paddock 4	
	Sheep	Goats	Sheep	Goats	Sheep	Goats	Sheep	Goats

6 1

7 3

8 2

9 18

10 24

Unit 14 MATHS: Problem Solving

1 $2.85

2 1 x $2, 2 x $1, 2 x 50c, 2 x 5c

Unit 15 English: Grammar & Punctuation

1 He

2 It

3 She

4 me

5 They

6 the <u>bear</u> and the <u>magic</u> <u>pot</u>
The Bear and the Magic Pot

7 <u>whales</u> and <u>other</u> <u>mammals</u>
Whales and Other Mammals

8 <u>australia's</u> <u>dinosaurs</u>
Australia's Dinosaurs

9 actor, acts

10 inventor, invents

11 narrator, narrates

12 director, directs

Unit 15 English: Phonic Knowledge & Spelling

1–10 Some questions may have more than one correct answer.

1 found

2 voice

3 fear

4 where

5 neighbour

6 mouth

7 toy

8 tear

9 stare

10 favourite

11 heard

12 hear

13 you

14 care

15 clear

Unit 15 English: Reading & Comprehension

1 a. a lost bird

2 c. It flew away when the cage door was open.

3 d. mauve

4 c. Benny

5 c. eat seeds from our hands

6 d. on the computer

7 a. click on the link

8 c. to identify the owner when it is found

9 b. in suburbs near Rosehill

10 Answers will vary. For example: keep the cage door closed.

Unit 16 MATHS: Number & Algebra

1 30, 31, 32, 33, 35. Counting F in 1s

2 60, 65, 70, 75, 85. Counting F in 5s

3 60, 50, 40, 30, 10. Counting B in 10s

4 42, 45, 48, 51, 57. Counting F in 3s

5 82, 80, 78, 76, 72. Counting B in 2s

6 139, 276, 342, 576, 854

ANSWERS

7 92, 209, 220, 902, 920

8 237, 364, 420, 546, 634

9 106, 160, 167, 170, 176

10 901, 919, 956, 965, 999

11 534

12 872

13 962

14 913

15  **16**   **1**

18 342

19 826

20 517

21 431

19 2 rows of 3 = 6, 3 columns of 2 = 6

20 3 rows of 4 = 12, 4 columns of 3 = 12

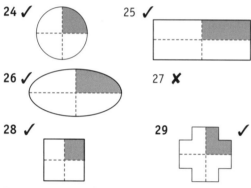

24 ✓   **25** ✓

26 ✓   **27** ✗

28 ✓   **29** ✓

30 2 toy cars each

31 3 blocks each

32 4 marbles each

Unit 16 MATHS: Measurement & Space

1 January

2 December

3 July

4 October

5 August

6 January

7 February

8 4

9 7

Unit 16 MATHS: Problem Solving

February 2020

Sunday	Monday	Tuesday	Wednesday	Thursday	Friday	Saturday
	1	2	3	4	5	6
7	8	9	10	11	12	13
14	15	16	17	18	19	20
21	22	23	24	25	26	27
28	29	30				

TERM 2 REVIEW

Term 2 English: Grammar & Punctuation

1 bear, honey, beehive

2 kangaroo, fence

3 Max, homework, Mr Ricci, morning

4 fear, mistake, girl, things

5 excitement, holidays, playground

6 helicopter, Sydney Harbour Bridge

7 tall, beautiful, front

8 happy, clever, magic

9 deep, tiny, hidden

10 frightened, big

11 silently	**16** ✓	**21** ✓
12 quickly	**17** ✗	**22** ✓
13 quietly	**18** ✓	**23** ✓
14 patiently	**19** ✗	**24** ✓
15 ✗	**20** ✓	

Term 2 English: Phonic Knowledge & Spelling

1 play	**15** dry	**29** ✗
2 brown	**16** glue	**30** ✓
3 glow	**17** pool	**31** ✓
4 look	**18** proud	**32** ✗
5 hoop	**19** astronaut	**33** ✗
6 blow	**20** Saturday	**34** ✓
7 paint	**21** birthday	**35** ✗
8 war	**22** where	**36** ✗
9 where	**23** pair	**37** ✓
10 cork	**24** pour	**38** ✓
11 burp	**25** ✓	**39** ✗
12 stare	**26** ✗	**40** ✓
13 here	**27** ✗	
14 you	**28** ✓	

TERM 2 MATHS: Number & Algebra

1 40, 50, 60, 70, 80. I am counting F in 10s

2 108, 110, 112, 114, 116. I am counting F in 2s

3 134, 133, 132, 131, 130. I am counting B in 1s

4 70, 75, 80, 85, 90, 95. I am counting F in 5s

5 82, 80, 78, 76, 74, 72. I am counting B in 2s

6 450, 550, 650, 750, 850, 950. I am counting F in 100s

7 3 hundreds, 5 tens, 4 ones = 354

8 5 hundreds, 2 tens, 7 ones = 527

9   **10**

11 2 rows of 3 = 6; 3 columns of 2 = 6

12 2 rows of 4 = 8; 4 columns of 2 = 8

13 a

Term 2 MATHS: Measurement & Space

1 square

2 kite

3 rectangle

4 triangle

5 rhombus

6 circle

TARGETING HOMEWORK 2 © PASCAL PRESS ISBN 9781925726442

7 **8**

Unit 17 English: Grammar & Punctuation

1 I saw <u>a</u> girl running down <u>the</u> street.
2 <u>The</u> cook at <u>the</u> café baked <u>a</u> big chocolate cake.
3 Mai had <u>a</u> party at <u>the</u> skate park for her birthday.
4 Tema had <u>an</u> apple and <u>an</u> orange in his lunch.
5 a
6 the, the
7 an, the
8 The, the
9 bat, car, helicopter, many, some
10 cake, fork, money, spoon, zoo

Unit 17 English: Phonic Knowledge & Spelling

1 shop, show, shape, shark, ship, shut, shack, shine
2 whine, white, when, what, whistle, wheel, whip, wheat
3 thing, thank, think, thistle, thirsty, thin, thorn, thick
4 chop, chat, chance, chime, champ, chain, cheese, chick
5 quad, quite, quick, quack, quilt, quip, quit, quid
6 black, sock, chick, check, thick, truck, rock, pluck

Unit 17 English: Reading & Comprehension

1 a. a berry and cream cake
2 b. by walking
3 c. because it was his wife's favourite
4 b. on the other side of town
5 a. His car wouldn't start.
6 b. He got lost.
7 b. He was tired from walking a long way.
8 d. There were no berry and cream cakes left.
9 b. disappointed
10 Answers will vary. For example, he might buy a different type of cake.

Unit 18 MATHS: Number & Algebra

1 20
2 3, 6, 9, 12, 15, 18, 21, 24
3 60
4 90
5 100, 200, 300, 400, 500, 600, 700, 800, 900, 1000
6 274, 275, 276, 277
7 275, 277, 279, 281
8 278, 283, 288, 293
9 283, 293, 303, 313
10 373, 473, 573, 673
11 973,
   9 hundreds, 7 tens, 3 ones

12 379,
   3 hundreds, 7 tens, 9 ones

13 4
14 3

Unit 18 MATHS: Measurement & Space

1 Toy bucket
2 Teaspoon
3 Glasses are half full.
4–10 Answers will vary. Students should begin to understand the idea of using the same unit of measurement (cup of water) to compare how much different containers hold.
11 cube
12 sphere
13 rectangular prism
14 cylinder
15 triangular prism
16 cone
17 pyramid

Unit 18 MATHS: Problem Solving

1 48   2 60

Unit 19 English: Grammar & Punctuation

1 John went to the beach and he had a swim.
2 The little girl fell over and she hurt her knee.
3–6 Answers will vary; sample answers provided.
3 The children went home and they did their homework.
4 The ball flew over the fence and the girl chased after it.
5 The dog barked loudly and the cat ran away.
6 I did my homework and then I played video games.
7 bee, butterfly, dragonfly, fly, ladybird
8 Earth, Jupiter, Mars, Mercury, Saturn

Unit 19 English: Phonic Knowledge & Spelling

1 screen, scratch, scrape, scream, scratchy, scram, screech, scrap
2 splendid, splendour, splat, split, splice, splinter, spleen, splutter
3 stretch, strap, strain, strip, stripe, strong, strange, straw
4 shrivel, shred, shrink, shrank, shriek, shrimp, shrunk, shrew
5 spree, spring, sprain, sprite, spread, sprouts, spray, sprinkle
6 shrimp
7 straw
8 sprinkle
9 splash
10 scratch

Unit 19 English: Reading & Comprehension

1 none
2 b. They both lay eggs.
3 c. Some hatch out of eggs and some are born live.
4 a. They live in water.
5 no
6 Almost all lizards have legs.
7 tortoises
8 d. freshwater crocodiles
9 a. One lays eggs and the other one doesn't.
10 b. saltwater crocodile

Unit 20 MATHS: Number & Algebra

1 226, 228, 230, 232, 236. Counting F in 2s
2 450, 445, 440, 435, 425. Counting B in 5s
3 315, 415, 515, 615, 815. Counting F in 100s
4 63, 53, 43, 33, 13. Counting B in 10s
5 262, 272, 282, 292, 312. Counting F in 10s
6 342, 345, 348, 351, 357. Counting F in 3s
7 29, 27, 25, 23, 19. Counting B in 2s
8 102, 103, 104, 105, 107. Counting F in 1s
9 699, 599, 499, 399, 199. Counting B in 100s
10 95, 100, 105, 110, 120. Counting F in 5s
11 972, 279
12 876, 678
13 321, 123
14 643, 346
15 954, 459
16 364
17 627
18 512
19 410
20 735
21 208
22 3 hundreds, 7 tens, 2 ones
23 4 hundreds, 6 tens, 5 ones
24 1 hundred, 9 tens, 3 ones
25 12, 6, 2
26 2 vases
27 5 children on each team

Unit 20 MATHS: Measurement & Space

1 quarter to 4
2 quarter to 8
3 quarter to 10
4 quarter to 1

5
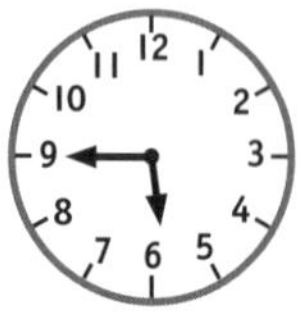
6
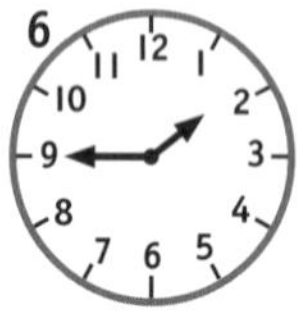
7
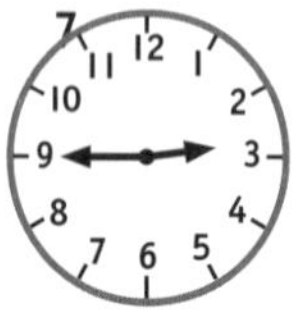
8
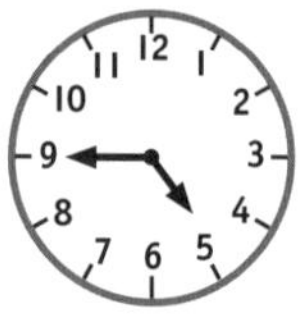
9
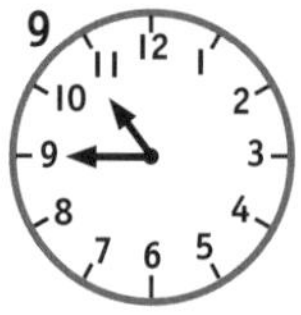
10
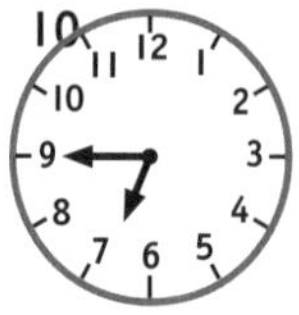
11
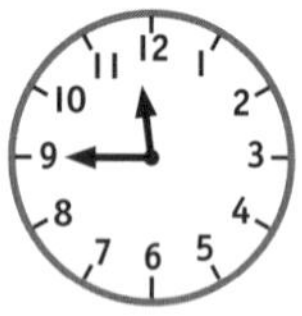
12
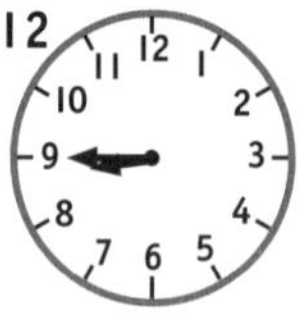

13 flip
14 slide
15 turn
16 turn
17 slide
18 slide

Unit 20 MATHS: Problem Solving

1 – everyone else was on their way **home** from town.

Unit 21 English: Grammar & Punctuation

1 John went to the beach but he didn't have a swim.
2 The little girl fell over but she didn't hurt herself.
3–5 Answers will vary; sample answers provided.
3 The children went home but no one was there.
4 The ball flew over the fence but no one chased after it.
5 I did my homework but then I had nothing to do.
7 dance, deep, dinner, door, dragon
8 lamb, lemur, lion, llama, lobster

Unit 21 English: Phonic Knowledge & Spelling

1 ear	4 tear	7 pear	10 hear	13 dear
2 clear	5 gear	8 wear	11 near	14 year
3 spear	6 shear	9 rear	12 fear	15 bear

16 match
17 stretch
18 witch
19 ditch
20 scratch
21 botch
22 fetch
23 catch
24 splotch
25 clutch
26 cure
27 measure
28 picture
29 mature
30 sure
31 pure
32 pleasure
33 treasure
34 mixture
35 capture

Unit 21 English: Reading & Comprehension

1 b. a shadow.
2 b. The way it grows.
3 c. because it always stays behind the boy
4 b. because of where the sun is in the sky
5 b. no
6 d. proud
7 c. There was no sun to make a shadow.
8 c. a ball
9 see; other answers will vary, for example: tree, free, he, bee.
10 way; other answers will vary, for example: day, say, ray, pay, tray.

Unit 22 MATHS: Number & Algebra

1	2	3	4	5	6	7	8	9	10
11	12	13	14	15	16	17	18	19	20
21	22	23	24	25	26	27	28	29	30
31	32	33	34	35	36	37	38	39	40
41	42	43	44	45	46	47	48	49	50
51	52	53	54	55	56	57	58	59	60
61	62	63	64	65	66	67	68	69	70
71	72	73	74	75	76	77	78	79	80
81	82	83	84	85	86	87	88	89	90
91	92	93	94	95	96	97	98	99	100

1 See grid above.
2 95, 90, 85, 80, 75, 70, 65, 60, 55, 50, 45, 40, 35, 30, 25, 20, 15, 10, 5
3 110, 115, 120, 125, 130, 135, 140, 145, 150, 155, 160, 165, 170, 175, 180, 185, 190, 195
4 See grid above.
5 15, 30, 45, 60, 75, 90
6 105
7 357, 375, 537, 573, 735, 753

TARGETING HOMEWORK 2 © PASCAL PRESS ISBN 9781925726442

8 468, 486, 648, 684, 846, 864
9 459, 495, 549, 594, 945, 954
10 123, 132, 213, 231, 312, 321
11 63
12 60 + 3
13 6 tens, 3 ones
14 40 + 14
15 30 + 24
16 20 + 34
17 10 + 44
18 60 + 15
19 50 + 25
20 40 + 35
21 30 + 45
22 20 + 55
23 347
24 300 + 40 + 7
25 3 hundreds, 4 tens, 7 ones
26 500 + 110 + 5
27 400 + 210 + 5
28 300 + 310 + 5
29 200 + 410 + 5
30 100 + 510 + 5
31 10, 10
32 5, 5
33 4, 4
34 2, 2

Unit 22 MATHS: Statistics

1 apple
2 5
3 1
4 2
5 6
6 kiwifruit
7 pears and oranges
8 oranges
9 plums
10 25

Unit 22 MATHS: Problem Solving

	A	B	C	D
6 and 4	6	4	10	2
3 and 7	7	3	10	4
8 and 2	8	2	10	6
1 and 9	9	1	10	8

A Counting forwards in 1s
B Counting backwards in 1s
C All 10
D Counting forwards in in 2s
    5 is missing frrom the tuble.

Unit 23 English: Grammar & Punctuation

1 It was raining so John didn't go to the beach.
2 Milo didn't come over so I watched TV by myself.
3–4 Answers will vary; sample answers provided.
3 I finished my homework so I went to the park.
4 The baby fell over so I picked her up.

5 gnat, goat, kite, know, lamb, nice
6 scamper, school, scrap, sign, singer

Unit 23 English: Phonic Knowledge & Spelling

1 knife
2 gnat
3 knee
4 wrap
5 know
6 hour
7 could
8 school
9 two
10 calf
11 sign
12 talk
13 bomb
14 limb
15 climb
16 tomb
17 lamb
18 crumb

Unit 23 English: Reading & Comprehension

1 b. warm-blooded mammals.
2 a. the temperature in and around the lion's body.
3 c. Make their own warmth.
4 b. no
5 d. 36–39 °C
6 97–103 °F
7 a. pink
8 d. blue
9 c. body
10 d. mane

Unit 24 MATHS: Number & Algebra

1 463
2 461
3 464
4 460
5 465
6 459
7 467
8 457
9 472
10 452
11 562
12 362
13 124, 64, 74, 334, 94, 104
14 329, 330, 339, 429
15 536, 537, 546, 636
16 495, 496, 505, 595

17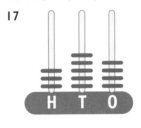
20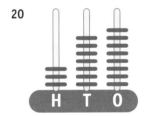
18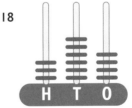
21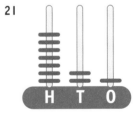
19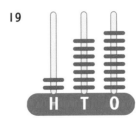
22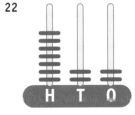

23 10, 10, no
24 5, 5, no
25 6, 6, yes, 2
26 5, 5, no
27 3, 3, no
28 3, 3, yes, 3

ANSWERS

29 ✓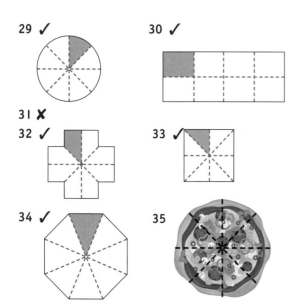

30 ✓

31 ✗

32 ✓

33 ✓

34 ✓

35

36 Each child should have 2 squares of chocolate.

Unit 24 MATHS: Measurement & Space

1 December
2 August
3 3
4 March, April, May
5 winter
6 June
7 February
8 autumn
9 spring

Unit 24 MATHS: Problem Solving

1   2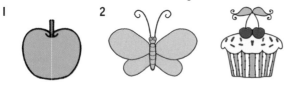

Term 3 English: Grammar & Punctuation

1 a, the
2 an, a
3 the, a
4 the, the, the
5 an, a, the
6 The shop was closed **so** Ari went home.
7 The baby was hungry **so** she started to cry.
8 Max looked everywhere **but** he couldn't find his book.
9 He turned off the light **and** went to sleep.
12 game, ghost, goat, gone, gust
13 knight, know, nice, night, nine

Term 3 English: Phonic Knowledge & Spelling

1 quilt
2 black
3 throne
4 shark
5 elephant
6 bling
7 strip
8 scratch

9 split
10 sprinkle
11 shriek
12 shrink
13–25 Last <u>year</u> I camped in a forest <u>near</u> the beach. One day I went for a walk. I didn't <u>wear</u> a raincoat because the sky was <u>clear</u>. I took all my <u>gear</u> in a backpack. When I had gone a short way, I could <u>hear</u> something strange. A <u>bear</u> cub was crying. There were <u>tears</u> on its face. I thought it might be hungry. I took a <u>pear</u> out of my backpack and gave it to the cub. Then I ran back to camp in <u>fear</u> that its mother might not be so sweet.
26 knife
27 two
28 bomb
29 gnat
30 sign

Term 3 MATHS: Number & Algebra

1 233, 235, 237, 241, 243. Counting in 2s
2 335, 345, 355, 375, 385. Counting in 10s
3 358, 458, 558, 758, 858. Counting in 100s
4 440, 445, 450, 460, 465. Counting in 5s
5 42, 45, 48, 54, 57. Counting in 3s
6 369, 396, 639, 693, 936, 963
7 578, 587, 758, 785, 857, 875
8 545
9 500 + 40 + 5
10 5 hundreds, 4 tens, 5 ones
11 256
12 200 + 50 + 6
13 2 hundreds, 5 tens, 6 ones
14 200 + 170 + 5
15 100 + 270 + 5
16 500 + 120 + 9
17 400 + 220 + 9
18 300 + 320 + 9
19 200 + 420 + 9
20 100 + 520 + 9
21 16, 4, 4
22 6, 6, no

Term 3 MATHS: Measurement & Space

1 half past 2	5 7 o'clock	9 half past 6
2 12 o'clock	6 3 o'clock	10 half past 9
3 quarter past 8	7 quarter to 4	
4 quarter past 1	8 quarter to 3	

Unit 25 English: Grammar & Punctuation

1 ill
2 laugh
3 joyful
4 lengthy
5 yell
6 small
7 young
8 smart
9 present

TARGETING HOMEWORK 2 © PASCAL PRESS ISBN 9781925726442

10 cook
11 garbage
12 jump
13 road
14 sleep
15 rock
16–20 Answers may vary; sample answers provided.
16 talk
17 quick
18 cold
19 mate, pal
20 right

Unit 25 English: Phonic Knowledge & Spelling

1 hic + cup	10 kitten	19 chisel
2 mag + net	11 rabbit	20 timber
3 pic + nic	12 hundred	21 into
4 rib + bon	13 rocket	22 using
5 hap + pen	14 hammer	23 hammer
6 but + ter	15 lazy	24 finger
7 bucket	16 opened	25 away
8 helmet	17 toolbox	
9 chicken	18 hammer	

Unit 25 English: Reading & Comprehension

1 b. Throw out some toys.
2 b. the ones he doesn't play with anymore
3 c. none of them
4 b. He liked them all.
5 d. everywhere
6 a. sort his toys.
7 d. disappointed
8 c. she thought he had too many toys
9 Answer depends on child's opinion.
10 Answers will vary.

Unit 26 MATHS: Number & Algebra

1 99, 102, 111, 392, 548, 627, 854, 909, 923, 990
2 906, 862, 694, 690, 623, 609, 428, 100, 99, 69
3 409, 499, 508, 510, 519, 609
4 327, 417, 426, 428, 437, 527
5 550, 640, 649, 651, 660, 750
6 245, 335, 344, 346, 355, 445
7 94, 184, 193, 195, 204, 294
8 243; 200 + 40 + 3; 2 hundreds, 4 tens, 3 ones
9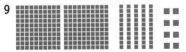
258; 200 + 50 + 8; 2 hundreds, 5 tens, 8 ones
10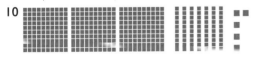
375; 300 + 70 + 5; 3 hundreds, 7 tens, 5 ones
11
192; 100 + 90 + 2; 1 hundreds, 9 tens, 2 ones
12 2, 1
13 4, 2
14 6, 3

15 8, 4
16 10, 5
17 12, 6
18 14, 7
19 16, 8
20 18, 9
21 20, 10
22 10 + 7 = 17
23 9 – 3 = 6
24 8 + 3 = 11

Unit 26 MATHS: Measurement & Space

1 bear	6 present	11 3, 2, 0
2 bus	7 8 blocks	12 5, 9, 6
3 plane	8 6, 12, 8	13 2, 1, 1
4 3 blocks	9 1, 0, 0	14 5, 8, 5
5 5 blocks	10 6, 12, 8	

Unit 26 MATHS: Problem Solving

1

1	2	3	4	5	6	7	8	9	10
11	12	13	14	15	16	17	18	19	20
21	22	23	24	25	26	27	28	29	30
31	32	33	34	35	36	37	38	39	40
41	42	43	44	45	46	47	48	49	50
51	52	53	54	55	56	57	58	59	60
61	62	63	64	65	66	67	68	69	70
71	72	73	74	75	76	77	78	79	80
81	82	83	84	85	86	87	88	89	90
91	92	93	94	95	96	97	98	99	100

2 They make a diagonal and get bigger by 9.
4 86
5 square
7 25

Unit 27 English: Grammar & Punctuation

1 ill
2 short
3 cry
4 sad
5 whisper
6 young
7 dry
8 left
9 save
10 easy
11 happy
12 dirty
13 quiet
14 fast
15 right
16–20 Answers may vary; sample answers provided.
16 enemy
17 rich, wealthy
18 bad
19 night
20 awake

ANSWERS

Unit 27 English: Phonic Knowledge & Spelling

1 fa/ther	5 a/bout	9 tiger
2 wa/ter	6 do/nate	10 scooter
3 mo/ment	7 robot	11 dragon
4 to/ken	8 spider	12 pilot

13–17 One syllable: act, book, branch, car, head

18–22 Two syllables: chuckle, dancer, funny, pizza, sometimes

23–27 More syllables: butterfly, carpenter, dragonfly, platypus, television

Unit 27 English: Reading & Comprehension

1 a. in alphabetical order
2 d. b. and c.
3 b. skeleton
4 c. They are covered in a special case.
5 pages 13–16 and 18
6 b. chrysalis
7 smell and feel
8 the structure that supports an animal's body
9 antennae
10 eyes

Unit 28 MATHS: Number & Algebra

1 Join these numbers in order: 22, 24, 26, 28, 30, 32, 34, 36, 38, 40, 52, 44, 46, 48, 50, 52, 54, 56, 22.
circle

2 Join these numbers in order: 55, 60, 65, 70, 75, 80, 85, 90, 95, 100, 105, 110, 115, 120, 55.
heart

3 Join these numbers in order: 150, 250, 350, 450, 550, 650, 750, 850, 150.
square

4 261
5 780
6 841
7 930

8 201
9 900
10 500 + 150 + 4
   400 + 250 + 4
   300 + 350 + 4
   200 + 450 + 4
11 600 + 190 + 3
   500 + 290 + 3
   400 + 390 + 3
   300 + 490 + 3
12 315
13 450
14 604
15 $4 \times 2 = 8, 2 \times 4 = 8$
16 $2 \times 6 = 12, 6 \times 2 = 12$
17 $3 \times 5 = 15, 5 \times 3 = 15$
18 $2 \times 3 = 6, 3 \times 2 = 6$
19 3×5
20 4×5

Unit 28 MATHS: Measurement & Space

1–4 Answers may vary; sample answers provided.

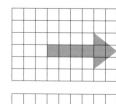
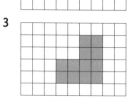

5 Thursday
6 Friday
7 30
8 1 April
9 19 April
10 11
11 Sunday
12 4
13 Wednesday
14 3 May

Unit 28 MATHS: Problem Solving

1   2   3

Unit 29 English: Grammar & Punctuation

1–10 Answers may vary; sample answers provided.

1 excited	11 happiness
2 sorry	12 pride
3 disappointed	13 disappointment
4 proud	14 anger
5 lonely	15 guilt
6 nervous	16 sorrow
7 confused	17 excitement
8 frightened	18 surprise
9 worried	19 confusion
10 tired	20 loneliness

Unit 29 English: Phonic Knowledge & Spelling

1 superhero	14 rattle + snake
2 sunflower	15 school + work
3 airport	16 space + ship
4 haircut	17 water + melon
5 grandmother	18 straw + berry
6 newspaper	19 tea + spoon
7 blueberry	20 brain + storm
8 candlestick	21 rainbow
9 sometimes	22 grandmother
10 moonlight	23 spaceship
11 mouse + trap	24 moonlight
12 light + house	25 lighthouse
13 rain + bow	

Unit 29 English: Reading & Comprehension

1 b. procedure
2 more than 2
3 d. paper and pencils
4 Draw a grid.
5 d. to win the most squares
6 a. by drawing the last side
7 d. both b. and c.
8 b. you may have another turn.
9 a. wins the most squares.
10 d. any number

Unit 30 MATHS: Number & Algebra

1 17, 87, 107, 297, 867
2 17, 70, 87, 107, 173, 297, 575, 670, 779, 867
3 46, 82, 120, 876, 292
4 999, 876, 643, 587, 475, 292, 123, 120, 82, 46
5 272; F in 3s
6 435; B in 5s
7 235; F in 100s
8 269; B in 100s

9 657; B in 10s

10 28, 30, 33, 38, 48, 148

11 82, 84, 87, 92, 102, 202

12 135, 137, 140, 145, 155, 255

13 257, 259, 262, 267, 277, 377

14   **15**   **16**

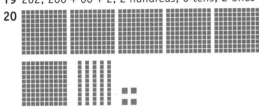

17 702

18 510

19 262; 200 + 60 + 2; 2 hundreds, 6 tens, 2 ones

20

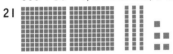

600 + 50 + 4; 6 hundreds, 5 tens, 4 ones

21

235; 2 hundreds, 3 tens, 5 ones

22

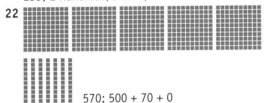

570; 500 + 70 + 0

23 4 hundreds + 2 tens + 5 ones
42 tens + 5 ones
4 hundreds + 25 ones

24 5 hundreds + 0 tens + 7 ones
50 tens + 7 ones
5 hundreds + 7 ones

25 4, 4

26 5, 5

27 $1, 50c

28 $5, 50c, 20c, 5c

29 $5, $2, 10c

30 $2, $2, 20c, 5c

Unit 30 MATHS: Statistics

1 Dog	3 5	5 2	7 Birds	9 4
2 Rat	4 Dogs	6 Mice	8 5	10 21

Unit 30 MATHS: Problem Solving

1 tray of 12 cookies, 12 trays of 1 cookie

2 trays of 6 cookies, 6 trays of 2 cookies

3 trays of 4 cookies, 4 trays of 3 cookies

Unit 31 English: Grammar & Punctuation

1 ✓	8 ✗	15 ✗	22 ✓
2 ✓	9 ✗	16 ✗	23 ✗
3 ✓	10 ✓	17 ✗	24 ✗
4 ✗	11 ✗	18 ✓	25 ✓
5 ✓	12 ✗	19 ✓	26 ✗
6 ✗	13 ✗	20 ✗	27 ✗
7 ✗	14 ✗	21 ✗	28 ✗

29–39

The day was hot, and the group had been walking for a long time. They were **exhausted**. The sun was starting to go down and they were **worried** that they wouldn't find somewhere to sleep before nightfall.

Many in the group began to grumble. Some of them were just **disappointed**, but Paige was **cross**. Dustin had told them **proudly** that he knew the way. Now that they were lost, Dustin was **embarrassed**.

Sarah told him not to **worry**, that they would find somewhere soon. Paige was **doubtful** and she wasn't ready to **forgive** him.

Soon Brand called out **excitedly**, "Look, there's a camping spot."

Dustin was **relieved**. "This is the camping spot we were looking for," he said. "We weren't lost after all."

40 relieved

41 pleased

42 embarrassed

43 happy

Unit 31 English: Phonic Knowledge & Spelling

1 starless	12 handwrite	23 firebreak
2 starlight	13 handstand	24 fireworks
3 starship	14 handover	25 airplane
4 starfish	15 handbook	26 airport
5 starfruit	16 handwork	27 aircraft
6 stardust	17 fireplace	28 airsick
7 starlike	18 firefighter	29 airbrush
8 stargaze	19 fireball	30 airmail
9 handball	20 firestorm	31 airhead
10 handbag	21 firebox	32 airplay
11 handshake	22 firehose	

Unit 31 English: Reading & Comprehension

1 c. letter

2 d. persuade

3 b. The Bear Family

4 a. Forgive her.

5 b. because she was hungry

6 a. frightened

7 b. sorry

8 b. Fix Baby Bear's chair.

9 Answers will vary.

10 Answers will vary.

Unit 32 MATHS: Number & Algebra

1 557, 657, 757, 857, 957

2 351, 361, 371, 381, 391

3 968, 958, 948, 938, 928

4 124, 123, 122, 121, 120

5 520, 525, 530, 535, 540

6 520, 610, 619, 621, 630, 720

7 799, 889, 898, 900, 909, 999

8 17, 107, 116, 118, 127, 217

9 205, 295, 304, 306, 315, 405

10 589, 598, 859, 895, 958, 985

11 26, 62, 206, 260, 602, 620

12 379, 397, 739, 793, 937, 973

13 +, 8 + 7 = 15

14 −, 16 − 6 = 10

15 –, $7 – $3 = $4
16 –, 14 – 3 = 11
17 2 × 6 = 12; 6 × 2 = 12
18 3 × 4 = 12; 4 × 3 = 12
19 9 ÷ 3 = 3 (3 flowers in each of 3 vases)

20 quarters	25 halves	30 2 cars each
21 eighths	26 8 cars each	31 2
22 eighths	27 8	32 one half
23 halves	28 4 cars each	
24 quarters	29 4	

Unit 32 MATHS: Statistics

1		
Car	😃😃😃😃😃😃😃😃😃😃😃😃😃	
Walk	😃😃😃😃😃😃😃😃😃	
Bicycle	😃😃😃😃	
Bus	😃😃	

2

12				
11				
10				
9				
8				
7				
6				
5				
4			■	
3			■	
2			■	■
1			■	■
	Car	Walk	Bicycle	Bus

3 How do you come to school most days?
4 Sample answers:
Most children come to school by car.
Fewer children come to school by bus.

Unit 32 MATHS: Problem Solving

1 C
2 B
3 A

TERM 4 REVIEW

Term 4 English: Grammar & Punctuation

1 difficult	5 shout	9 tall
2 happy	6 everyone	10 future
3 old	7 ask	
4 depart	8 careful	

11–17 Answers may vary; sample answers provided.

11 frightened	14 frustrated	17 shy
12 jealous	15 grumpy	
13 bored	16 angry	

Term 4 English: Phonic Knowledge & Spelling

1 pa/per	15 3	29 earring
2 be/cause	16 2	30 catfish
3 o/pen	17 2	31 laptop
4 car/rot	18 2	32 bookmark
5 but/ter	19 2	33 ringside
6 cle/ver	20 1	34 snowman
7 but/ton	21 3	35 hotdog
8 man/ner	22 1	36 raincoat
9 pen/cil	23 2	37 snowman
10 pla/net	24 4	38 hotdog
11 3	25 2	39 laptop
12 2	26 suitcase	40 suitcase
13 1	27 notebook	41 notebook
14 1	28 raincoat	

Term 4 MATHS: Number & Algebra

1 978 circled, 197 crossed
2 197, 302, 345, 420, 432, 507, 625, 750, 864, 978
3 208
4 580
5 800 + 50 + 1 or 8 hundreds, 5 tens, 1 one
6 500 + 90 + 7 or 5 hundreds, 9 tens, 7 ones
7 200 + 30 or 2 hundreds, 3 tens, 0 ones
8 400 + 9 or 4 hundreds, 0 tens, 9 ones
9 2 × 5 = 10
10 8 ÷ 4 = 2
11 8 – 4 = 4
12 6 + 4 = 10

13   14   15

Term 4 MATHS: Measurement & Space

1 3

2–7

8 flip
9 turn
10 slide

Term 4 MATHS: Statistics

1 Tema ||||| ||||| ||| Sasha ||||| ||||| ||||| |||
Li ||||| || Zayne

2–3 Sample questions and answers:
Who scored the most runs? Sasha
Who scored the least runs? Zayne
How many more runs did Sasha make than Tema? 5